Parsely

Jared A. Sorensen

CREDITS

Writing and game design: Jared A. Sorensen
Editing: Patrick Riegert, Elisa Mader and Dixie Cochran
Graphic Design and Layout: Radek Drozdalski and Luke Crane
Project Manager: Nathan Black

Artists
Jordan Worley (cover art)
Rebekie Bennington (maps and GUI pixel art)
Manning L. Krull (*Action Castle* series, *Jungle Adventure, Spooky Manor*)
Alice K. Hansmann (*Blackboard Jungle*)
Ariel ZB (*Dangertown Beatdown*)
Lukas Wong-Achorn (*Dangertown Beatdown* map and pixel art portraits)
Todd James (*Flaming Goat!*)
"Calamity" Jon Morris (*Pumpkin Town*)
Keith Senkowski (*Six-Gun Showdown*)
Alexey Andreyev (*Space Station*)
Sam Araya (*Z-Ward*)

Foreword
Peter Adkison

Playtesters
Ashley Banks, Joe Ceirante, Luke Crane, Radek "FROZ" Drozdalski, Angela Fagg, Nicole Fitting, Joss Hansmann, Wei-Hwa Huang, James Jelkin, Jim Jones, Shay Lehmann, Chris LoPresto, Megan McFerren, Topi Makkonen, Christopher R. Marshall, Thor Olavsrud, Terry Romero, Max Saltonstall and the Parsely players at Google, John Stavropoulos, Brian Tannenbaum, Mayuran Tiruchelvam, David Turner and all Parsely fans, Parsers, players and podcasters everywhere!

Special Thanks
Joss Hansmann for love and support; Luke Crane, Thor Olavsrud and Radek Drozdalski for BEING ON FIRE; J. Florio for playing Flaming Goat! with me on the 7 train; Andy Kitkowski, Mike Bracken and Sean and Noriko Sakamoto for katakana and J-horror expertise; the Charles Hayden Planetarium staff for hosting Space Station at the Museum of Science in 2016 and to Rob Nelson for being my pre-show guinea pig; Andrew Looney for carrying the torch at conventions; James Jelkin, Madison Coppola, Brian León, Regina Hernandez and Thomas Countz for making me look good on camera for my Kickstarter video and to all those who backed this book.

Last but not least, thanks to Michael Lipinski and Steven Meretzky. This is all your fault!

```
]CATALOG
DISK VOLUME 254
 A 004 HELLO
 I 006 README
*B 015 ACTION CASTLE
*B 029 ACTION CASTLE II
*B 047 ACTION CASTLE III
*B 075 BLACKBOARD JUNGLE
*B 085 DANGERTOWN BEATDOWN
*B 116 FLAMING GOAT
*B 119 JUNGLE ADVENTURE
*B 139 PUMPKIN TOWN
*B 167 SIX-GUN SHOWDOWN
*B 193 SPACE STATION
*B 213 SPOOKY MANOR
*B 241 Z-WARD
*T 270 INDEX
]RUN PARSELY
```

HELLO

Around the turn of the century, the world of roleplaying games was turned upside down with what's generally referred to as the rise of "indie roleplaying games." Was it a reaction to the runaway popularity of Dungeons & Dragons–like products in the wake of the Open Game License? Or was Y2K some sort of psychic vibration instead of a technoglitch? One thing was clear: a new breed of game designer was quietly engineering a revolution in RPG design, and at the heart of this scene was Jared Sorensen.

When I met Jared he hadn't yet conceived the Parsely line, but I was already a big fan of his games: *Lacuna Part I*, a game of shadowy corporations and aliens in a nightmare space, and *InSpectres*, a riff on the *Ghostbusters* movie that's still one of my go-to games when I'm asked to run an RPG. And, of course, I'm still a fan of *FreeMarket*, which Jared codesigned with Luke Crane.

Then, in 2009, Jared published the first Parsely game: *Action Castle*. It was the introduction to a series of games that presented a completely new and original play style: players would take turns calling

out commands normally reserved for the keyboard of 1980s-era text-adventure games. And if one of those players gave an illegal or unintelligible command, the game master would yell out an appropriate—and often sarcastic—error message.

Somehow, this reversal of a face-to-face RPG—arguably based on pen-and-paper RPGs like Dungeons & Dragons—managed to create a fun, zany and very social group play experience. Even better, this game worked with a lot of people. I believe Jared has run the game for a hundred players or more at one time.

Parsely could be the most interesting party game ever designed. And it was created by one of the most fascinating designers I've ever met and am pleased to call my friend.

—Peter D. Adkison

Valentine's Day, 2017

README

Parsely games are based on the old text-adventure parsers from the late 1970s and early 1980s—games such as *Colossal Cave Adventure*, *Zork* and *Planetfall*. In this version, a person replaces the computer, and a map and script replace the software.

One person (most likely you) is the Parser, the name given to the program that runs a text adventure. It's your job to relay the game world to the players. You describe what the character sees, the results of their actions and anything else appearing in the game. You also keep track of the character's current location, inventory and score. Refer to yourself as "I" when talking to the players.

Everyone else playing the game shares one character. Refer to each player as "you" during the game. You need at least two humans to play a Parsely game: a Parser and a player. There's no limit to the number of players, making Parsely games ideal for parties, conventions and other large gatherings of geeks who are into this kind of thing.

Action Castle was created in 2003, on the fly, at a friend's party. Years later, I'd often bring it with me to game conventions, first with 30 players, then 60, then 200, and eventually over 400! My pal and fellow game designer, Luke Crane, persuaded me to publish it as a Z-fold pamphlet in 2009. Now it's time to delve back into the source code, recompile it all and bundle it together for this book.

Would you like to play a game (Y/N)?

—Jared Sorensen

April Fools' Day, 2017

HOW IT WORKS

The first step is to welcome the players—sound effects and extravagant gestures are optional. Descriptions and other text to be read aloud to the players is in black, like this text. Information for the Parser (that is not to be read directly to the players) is in blue. Sometimes the blue text indicates the room or object, other times the > symbol will precede a longer description.

So, after starting the game with a warm welcome...

"Welcome to Action Castle!"

...proceed by describing the starting room, its contents and its exits:

You are standing in a small cottage. There is a fishing pole here. A door leads outside.

> Sometimes the description of a room will change because of the players' actions. For example, when an object is taken, omit that object from the room's description.

After the players visit the same room a few times, feel free to go into BRIEF mode and limit your description to just the name of the room. Be as helpful or as vague as you wish. If the players use the LOOK command, repeat the room's full description, with exits.

Turns & Time

Each player gets to take a turn to give a command—usually a one-word or two-word action in this format: {verb} {noun}.

Examples:

GO WEST, TAKE KEY, CLIMB TREE, SMELL ROSE or WEAR CROWN

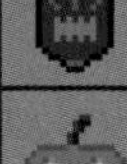

You may allow similar phrases at your discretion. SNIFF ROSE and CLIMB UP are fine. INHALE ROSE'S SCENT and SHIMMY UP TREE, not so much.

Sometimes you'll need more information from the player making the command. Anything you ask may be answered by the current player, as in the following example:

CATCH FISH: What do you want to use to catch a fish?

FISHING POLE: You catch a fish!

Feel free to allow more complex commands—as long as players don't go overboard (i.e., don't allow "then" or "and" commands)—such as:

CATCH FISH WITH FISHING POLE

Unless a player is questioning a character, commands should be statements:

CAN I GO WEST? I dunno! Can you?

Characters may be addressed by using the format {character}, {question}; or by using ASK {character} ABOUT {topic}, as in the following two examples:

PRINCESS, CAN YOU LEAVE THIS TOWER? The princess shakes her head no.

ASK PRINCESS ABOUT THE KING: "Father died several years ago. They say his restless spirit still haunts this castle."

When a player examines an object or character, read them the description or make one up if it's not important to the puzzle. You can also be vague, play dumb or crack wise:

EXAMINE POND: You see fish swimming below the pond's surface.

EXAMINE POLE: The fishing pole consists of a stick, some string and a hook.

EXAMINE HOOK: It's a hook...a plot hook. *twirls mustache*

Once all the players have taken a turn, loop back to the first player and continue until the players win, time expires or everyone gets mad and goes home. Turns aren't the only factor they need to worry about! Each game should last no more than 60–90 minutes. Failing to complete the game within the allotted time span results in a "Game Over" and final score.

Objects

Objects that may be taken by the players are underlined when first mentioned. When taken, they're stored in the player inventory. Unless it is otherwise noted, players have unlimited space to carry objects. Some objects may also be worn.

TAKE POLE: You now have the fishing pole.

GET STRING: That cannot be removed.

INVENTORY: You are carrying a fishing pole, a crown and a lamp.

> A handy inventory checklist is included with each game.

WEAR CROWN: You are now wearing the crown.

Basic Commands

Every Parsely game shares a few basic commands. They're used to travel the map and to interact with rooms, objects and characters. In the text, they are written in all caps.

Direction

EXIT, ENTER, LEAVE, BACK, EAST, WEST, NORTH, SOUTH, UP and DOWN.

A player can also use GO {direction}. Some games may allow other directions, such as NORTHWEST.

LEAVE, EXIT, OUT or BACK may be used only in rooms with one exit.

Perception

LOOK, EXAMINE, SEARCH, SMELL, LISTEN, TASTE and TOUCH.

LOOK will repeat a room's description, contents and exits.

LOOK {exit} will give a player a glimpse into what lies beyond the exit.

EXAMINE {object} or EXAMINE {character} gives a player a description of that object or character. Commands such as SMELL or LISTEN may yield a response only in certain situations.

Interaction

TAKE, GET, DROP, TALK, KILL, LIGHT, WEAR, USE, etc.

Remember, as the Parser, you're portraying a personal computer from the 1980s with an 8-bit processor. If players issue commands that are nonsensical or complex or that use unusual words, respond appropriately:

EAT FISHING POLE: You can't eat that!

GO FISH: You can't go that way.

TALK TO TREE: The tree has no desire to chat with you.

CAST THE POLE: You don't know that spell.

PUT WORM ON HOOK AND CATCH A FISH WITH IT: What?

HELLO: Hi.

Special Commands

Some commands are used to interact with the Parsely game system itself:

HELP lists these special system commands: HELP, INVENTORY, SAVE, LOAD/RELOAD/RESTORE, RESTART/RESET, SCORE and QUIT.

INVENTORY lists all objects worn or carried. In games with lots of objects, this list can be quite long, so take notes or have a good memory!

SAVE stores the player character's current location, inventory and status. If the player character dies, LOAD, RELOAD or RESTORE returns them to their last save point. SAVE always overwrites the previous save point, and players are limited to three saves unless otherwise noted in the text. Whenever the players save, be sure to let them know how many saves they have left!

RESTART ends the current game and starts over from the beginning.

SCORE lets the players know how they're doing. This is usually a number between 0 and 100, based on their accomplishments (such as items picked up, puzzles solved or enemies defeated).

QUIT ends the game!

CONDITIONAL EXITS

Not all exits are immediately accessible or even visible. These exits are marked with an alert symbol (⊡). They may be hidden, blocked or locked. Some require a specific command or inventory item. They also may be opened by events that are triggered during the game. Details about these exits are listed in the room description. When you see this symbol in front of the room exit be sure to check the appropriate room description before proceeding.

WINNING & LOSING

All Parsely games have a victory condition that ends the game. Although it may be a long and difficult journey, playing the game as designed should always bring the players to an ending—either a loss or a win. Every situation has an out, even if it's fatal! There are no hopeless games.

A flawless victory usually results in a score of 100/100 points. Some games may be completed even if the players haven't earned every point possible.

For example:

SIT ON THRONE: You sit on the throne. The people cheer your name, welcoming you as their new ruler. THE END. Congratulations—your score is 99/100!

Players lose when their character is killed by monsters, traps or foolish actions such as JUMP OFF CLIFF. When this happens, announce that they've died and tell them their final score. Then, ask if they wish to restart the game, as in the following example:

ATTACK TROLL: The troll is much mightier than you, and your attack does little to harm it. In response, it tears you limb from limb. You have died. THE END. Thanks for playing! Your score is 15/100. Would you like to restart the game?

If the players saved the game at any point, give them the option to reload should they meet their demise:

KILL ME: You have died. THE END. Thanks for playing! Your score is 15/100. Would you like to reload from your saved game?

BELLS & WHISTLES

Parsely games are puzzles, but also a kind of performance art. Think of each game like a nerdy version of karaoke—it's more about entertaining the crowd than singing well.

As the Parser, you run the show, interpret commands and give feedback in the form of information, challenges and comedy. This is easier than you might think! Here are some tips:

Be cruel but fair.

One of the great things about text adventures (and a reason why they're remembered so fondly) is that the puzzles were annoying but logical, and the Parser was simple but reliable. Don't coddle the players by allowing sloppy grammar, complex commands or dumb jokes. Respond the way a sarcastic computer would. If a player issues a proper command but at the wrong time, give them a clue:

MARRY PRINCESS: The princess will only marry royalty.

The players now know that MARRY PRINCESS is an acceptable command, but only if they figure out how to become royalty. Compare that to this exchange:

KISS PRINCESS: *slap* I'm not that kind of girl!

The princess lets the players know that she's just not that into the player character. When this happens in my games, I slap my own hand and do my "princess voice." It doesn't affect the outcome of the game, but it always gets laughs.

Be loud…

Speak up, especially when playing Parsely games with a large group or in a noisy environment. This is no time to be a wallflower! You need to be heard above the din. This doesn't mean you have to guarantee all the players are paying attention—

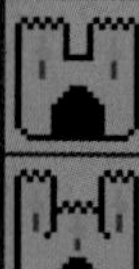

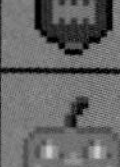

that's on them. It just means you need to speak loudly enough to be heard.

Listen!
Most of the comedy actually comes from the players. Their expectations colliding with your results generate a lot of humor. You don't have to wink at the crowd, tell jokes or clown around. Just listen to what a player says to you. If there's any room for misunderstanding, irony or humor, take advantage of it. In my experience, gestures, funny voices and sound effects go a long way to make the game come alive:

TAKE PRINCESS: *slap* I'm not that kind of girl!

Be consistent.
The hardest thing to do is to keep track of everything. The game works best when you can do it all from memory, without writing down notes or consulting maps or game rules. So learn it! And when you do, be consistent in your responses to the player. Every action has a reaction:

A valid response:

TAKE KEY: You now have the key.

A question:

USE KEY: How do you want to use the key?

A syntax error:

MAKE A COPY OF THE KEY: I don't know how to "make a copy."

Or something funny and/or rude:

WHAT DOES THE KEY LOOK LIKE?: It looks like a key, dummy.

Oh, and of course…
HAVE FUN: I don't understand how to "have fun."

Your greatest challenge lies ahead–and downward.

The original Parsely game! Explore the lands of Action Castle, brave its dangers and claim the throne!

CONTENT RATED BY MMTRB

FANTASY

BEGINNER

EVERYONE (10+)

ACTION CASTLE MAP

TOWER
TOWER STAIRS
GREAT FEASTING HALL
COURTYARD
THRONE ROOM
DUNGEON STAIRS
DUNGEON

COTTAGE

MENU

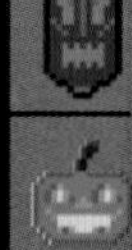

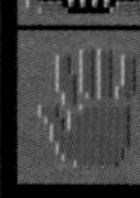

You are standing in a small cottage. There is a fishing pole here. A door leads outside.

Every new game starts in the Cottage. The player also starts the game with a lamp, although the **INVENTORY** command must be invoked to learn this information. To help newbies, you can add the lamp to the description of the Cottage at the start of the game.

EXAMINE LAMP: You see an old lamp; it's currently unlit.

> The player may only LIGHT the lamp when it's too dark to see.

EXAMINE FISHING POLE: You see a simple fishing pole.

COTTAGE exits are:

> OUT page 18 GARDEN PATH

GARDEN PATH

You're on a lush garden path that leads north and south. There is a rosebush here. There is a cottage here.

EXAMINE ROSEBUSH: You find a single red rose.

> The player can SMELL, GET, TAKE or PICK the rose.

GARDEN PATH exits are:

> NORTH page 19 WINDING PATH
> SOUTH page 19 FISH POND
> ENTER page 18 COTTAGE

FISH POND

You are at the edge of a fish pond. A path leads north.

USE FISHING POLE: You catch a wriggling fish!

> The player cannot eat the fish—it's raw!

FISH POND exits are:

> NORTH page 18 GARDEN PATH

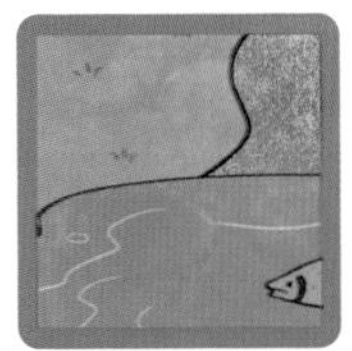

WINDING PATH

You are walking along a winding path that leads south and east. There is a tall tree here.

CLIMB TREE/UP: You climb up the tree—it takes a long time.

> While in the tree, the player can EXAMINE, BREAK or TAKE the dead branch:

You are at the top of a tall tree. There is a stout dead branch here. From your perch you can see the tower of Action Castle.

CLIMB TREE/DOWN: You climb down the tree—it takes a long time.

> Players who JUMP will not survive the fall.

EXAMINE DEAD BRANCH: You think it would make a good club.

> If used to HIT or CLUB something, the dead branch breaks and cannot be used again.

WINDING PATH exits are:

> SOUTH page 18 GARDEN PATH

> EAST page 20 DRAWBRIDGE

DRAWBRIDGE

You come to the drawbridge of Action Castle. There is a mean troll guarding the bridge.

CROSS BRIDGE: The troll blocks your path.

EXAMINE TROLL: The troll has a warty green hide and looks hungry.

> If the player lingers for more than two or three moves, the troll will kill them. The troll will also rip limb from limb anyone who attacks it. It will not leave this spot unless given a raw fish, at which point it will run off to eat its prize.

DRAWBRIDGE exits are:

> WEST page 19 WINDING PATH

☒ EAST page 21 COURTYARD

COURTYARD

You are in the courtyard of Action Castle. A castle guard stands watch to the east. Stairs lead up into the tower and down into darkness.

> If the player is wearing the crown:

The guard drops to his knee and bows deeply. "My liege. Your public awaits you in the throne room."

EXAMINE GUARD: The guard wears chainmail armor but no helmet. A key hangs from his belt.

> The player may not go east until the guard is unconscious. The guard blocks the eastern exit. The player may HIT the guard with the branch to knock him out. The guard's key may then be taken.

COURTYARD exits are:

☒ EAST page 25 GREAT FEASTING HALL

> WEST page 20 DRAWBRIDGE

> UP page 22 TOWER STAIRS

> DOWN page 22 DUNGEON STAIRS

MENU

TOWER STAIRS

You climb the tower stairs until you come to a door.

OPEN DOOR: The door is locked.

> The player must use the guard's key to UNLOCK DOOR. Once the door is unlocked, the player may GO IN or GO UP to the Tower, or go DOWN to the Courtyard.

TOWER STAIRS exits are:

⊡ IN or UP page 23 TOWER

> DOWN page 21 COURTYARD

DUNGEON STAIRS

You are on the dungeon stairs. It's very dark here.

GO DOWN: It's too dark to see!

> Fortunately, there are no grues nearby.

LIGHT CANDLE: The candle's flickering flame is blown out by a draft.

LIGHT LAMP: You can now see well enough to continue down the stairs.

> The player is free to continue downstairs.

DUNGEON STAIRS exits are:

> UP page 21 COURTYARD

⊡ DOWN page 24 DUNGEON

TOWER

You are in the tower. There is a princess here. Stairs lead down.

EXAMINE PRINCESS: The princess is beautiful, sad and lonely.

> The player may TALK to the princess. She will only respond once given the rose. Then she'll warm up to the player but will not allow herself to be kissed, touched or removed from this room unless the player has the crown.

MARRY PRINCESS: "You're not royalty!"

ASK PRINCESS ABOUT GHOST: "The guards whisper that the ghost of the king haunts the dungeons as a restless spirit!"

ASK ABOUT CROWN: "My father's crown was lost after he died."

ASK ABOUT TOWER: "I cannot leave the tower until I'm wed!"

ASK ABOUT THRONE: "Only the rightful ruler of Action Castle may claim the throne!"

GIVE CROWN TO PRINCESS: "My father's crown! You have put his soul to rest and may now take his place as ruler of this land!" She places the crown on your head.

> The crowned player may then PROPOSE or MARRY PRINCESS and she will accept. The player's gender is irrelevant. Once married, she will leave the tower with the player. This isn't required to beat the game, but it's fun and gives the player bonus points.

TOWER exits are:

> DOWN page 22 TOWER STAIRS

DUNGEON

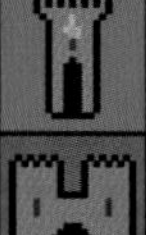

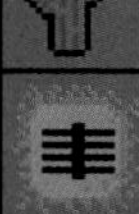

You are in the dungeon. There is a spooky ghost here. Stairs lead up.

EXAMINE GHOST: The ghost has bony, claw-like fingers and wears a gold crown.

EXAMINE CROWN: You see the gold crown that once belonged to the king of Action Castle.

> Each turn spent in the Dungeon causes the ghost to drift closer and closer. If not defeated within three turns, the ghost reaches out a skeletal hand and drains the player's life force. THE END.

> The player must possess the candle from the Great Feasting Hall to defeat the ghost.

LIGHT CANDLE: The strange candle gives off a strange, acrid smoke, causing the ghost to flee the dungeon. It leaves behind a gold crown.

> The player can then take the crown. It must first be given to the princess before it can be worn.

DUNGEON exits are:

> UP page 22 DUNGEON STAIRS

GREAT FEASTING HALL

You stand inside the great feasting hall. There is a strange candle here. Exits are to the east and west.

> If the player is wearing the crown, this hall will be full of people.

The people gathered here raise a toast to their new ruler!

EXAMINE CANDLE: You see that the strange candle is covered in mysterious runes.

READ RUNES: The odd runes are part of an exorcism ritual used to dispel evil spirits.

LIGHT CANDLE: The candle casts a flickering flame and emits acrid smoke.

> If the player walks down the Dungeon Stairs with the lit candle, the draft in the stairwell will blow out the candle. It will remain lit in the Dungeon long enough to dispel the spooky ghost.

GREAT FEASTING HALL exits are:

> EAST page 26 THRONE ROOM

> WEST page 21 COURTYARD

THRONE ROOM

This is the throne room of Action Castle. There is an ornate gold throne here.

> If the player is wearing the crown, the room is full of people.

The people gathered here cheer and applaud as you enter!

EXAMINE THRONE: You see an ornate gold throne.

> The player may CLAIM THRONE or SIT ON THRONE, but only while wearing the gold crown.

SIT ON THRONE: You are now the new ruler of Action Castle! THE END.

> The player then wins the game. See the Scoring section (page 27).

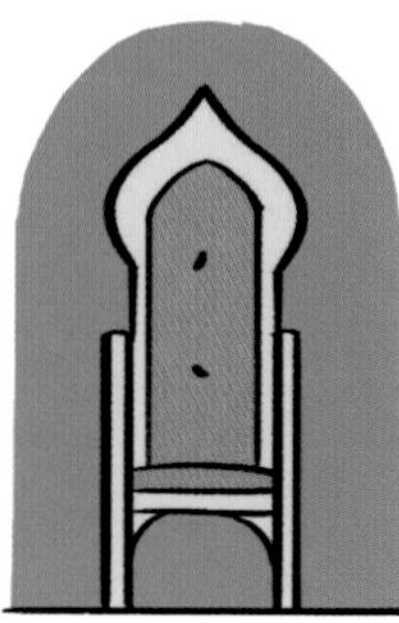

THRONE ROOM exits are:

> WEST page 25 GREAT FEASTING HALL

INVENTORY CHECKLIST

These items may be carried by the player:

- ☒ Lamp
- ☐ Fishing pole
- ☐ Rose
- ☐ Fish
- ☐ Branch
- ☐ Key
- ☐ Candle
- ☐ Crown

SCORING

The players can earn a maximum of 100 points:

Each location visited . . . . +2 (total of 24 points)
Each item collected. . . . . +5 (total of 35 points)
Defeating the troll. . . . . +10
Defeating the guard . . . . +10
Defeating the ghost . . . . +10
Proposing to the princess . . . . +5
Claiming the throne . . . . +5
Finishing without saving . . . . +1

EXAMPLE OF PLAY

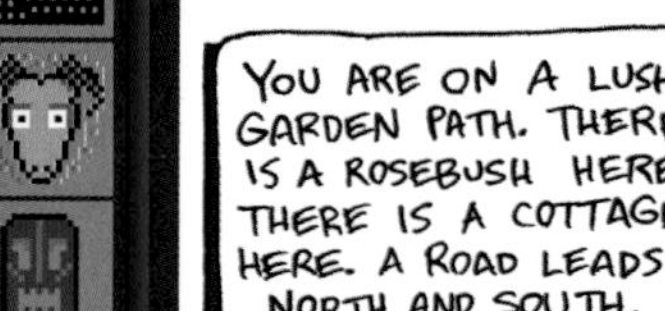

The next step downward to danger.

Return to Action Castle

Many years have passed since the king of Action Castle was crowned. Now, a simple cobbler with dreams of fortune and glory sets out on a grand adventure.

CONTENT RATED BY MMTRB

ACTION CASTLE II MAP

ACTION CASTLE
COURTYARD
THRONE ROOM
IN THE MOAT
DUNGEON STAIRS
DUNGEON
UNDERGROUND
TREASURE TROVE

MENU

COBBLER'S WORKSHOP

You are in your workshop. A pair of velvet slippers is here. A door leads outside.

> The player character starts the game with a shiny copper penny.

EXAMINE SLIPPERS: You see a pair of fine purple velvet slippers fit for a king.

WEAR SLIPPERS: The slippers don't fit.

COBBLER'S WORKSHOP exits are:

> OUT page 32 TOWN SQUARE

TOWN SQUARE

It's a dark, cold night. Exits lead north, south, east and west. You see a wishing well here.

EXAMINE WELL: Well, well. A well! It's made of stone, and it's made rather well.

DROP PENNY IN WELL: You drop the penny into the well and hear a faint *plink* as it hits the bottom. There goes your last cent. Now what?

LOOK NORTH: You see your shop.

LOOK SOUTH: You see the smithy.

LOOK EAST: You see a road leading out of town.

LOOK WEST: You see the town hall.

TOWN SQUARE exits are:

> NORTH page 32 COBBLER'S WORKSHOP
> SOUTH page 34 SMITHY
> EAST page 34 OLD POND ROAD
> WEST page 33 TOWN HALL

TOWN HALL

You are in the town hall. Rosemary, the mayor's daughter, is here.

EXAMINE ROSEMARY: Hey, it's your girlfriend! She's a sweet girl, but she's painfully shy. Rosemary blushes as she catches you looking at her.

> Feel free to change Rosemary to Sage, the player character's boyfriend.

ASK ROSEMARY TO FOLLOW: Rosemary says it's too chilly to go outside.

> Rosemary will follow the player character once she has the blanket.

GIVE BLANKET TO ROSEMARY: Rosemary kisses you on the cheek and drapes the blanket over her shoulders.

GIVE RING or PROPOSE: You want to propose here? Maybe a more romantic location is in order?

TOWN HALL exits are:

> OUT page 32 TOWN SQUARE

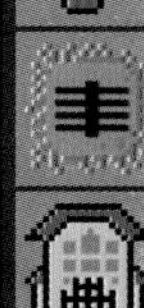

SMITHY

You are in the smithy. The blacksmith is at the forge, hammering on some red-hot iron. There is a grindstone here.

EXAMINE GRINDSTONE: If you would just put your nose to it, you might make something of yourself. For now, you're stuck being a cobbler.

EXAMINE SMITH: You see a burly, bearded man. He snorts, "Whaddya want? I'm busy!"

SHARPEN AXE: You have no idea how to sharpen an axe.

GIVE AXE TO SMITH: The smith mutters under his breath and sharpens the axe for you. You now have a sharp axe.

SMITHY exits are:

> OUT page 32 TOWN SQUARE

OLD POND ROAD

You're walking down Old Pond Road, a wide cobblestone road that used to be lined with rosebushes. There is a sign here. Old Pond Road runs north to south. The town is to the east.

READ SIGN: You see a weather-beaten sign that reads, "Please don't pick the roses."

OLD POND ROAD exits are:

> NORTH page 37 BEND IN THE ROAD
> SOUTH page 35 OLD POND
> WEST page 32 TOWN SQUARE

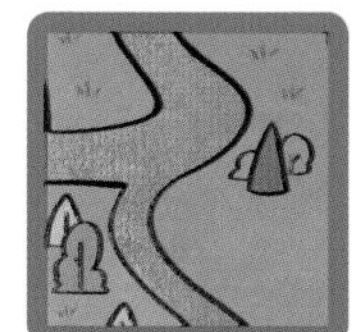

OLD POND

You stand at the edge of the old pond. The clear night sky above is full of stars. You see a rowboat here. A path runs alongside the pond to the north and south.

> If Rosemary/Sage followed the player character here, they won't go any farther south.

EXAMINE BOAT: You see that the boat is in fair condition. It contains a blanket.

EXAMINE BLANKET: You see the blanket is made of fine wool. It looks warm.

ENTER BOAT: You're now in the boat.

ROW BOAT: Row, row, row your boat. Life is but a dream. You row out to the middle of the pond. It's quiet, peaceful and romantic here.

> Once in the middle of the pond, a player must row back to shore to exit the boat.

> A player with the ring can GIVE RING or PROPOSE to Rosemary/Sage:

Your beloved kisses you on the cheek, exclaiming, "Of course I do!" The two of you return to town and live happily ever after. THE END.

OLD POND exits are:
> NORTH page 34 OLD POND ROAD
> SOUTH page 36 HERMIT'S CAVE

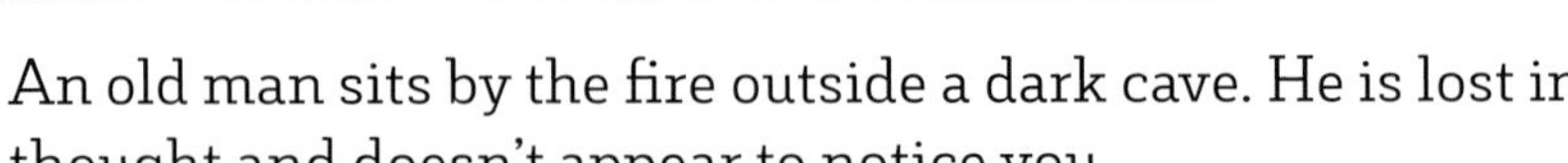

HERMIT'S CAVE

An old man sits by the fire outside a dark cave. He is lost in thought and doesn't appear to notice you.

> If the player character arrives here via the chute in the Treasure Trove, the hermit will be long gone.

EXAMINE OLD MAN: It's just some crazy old hermit. He's bearded, barefoot and dirty. His only clothing is a burlap sack tied about his waist with a piece of rope.

TALK TO HERMIT: The hermit mumbles something about a prophecy, then goes back to staring into the fire.

TALK TO HERMIT ABOUT PROPHECY: The hermit turns away from the fire and intones, "A champion will arise from humble beginnings to bring peace to the land."

GIVE SLIPPERS TO HERMIT: The hermit accepts your gift and gives you this bit of advice: "Remember, only a fool desires wealth and power. The wise person has everything they need." He taps his head and gives you a sly wink.

> The hermit isn't interested in anything else in the player character's possession.

ENTER CAVE: It's too dark and scary in there. Also: It smells.

HERMIT'S CAVE exits are:

> NORTH page 35 OLD POND

BEND IN THE ROAD

You arrive at a bend in the road. There is an old tree stump here. You see Action Castle to the east.

> If Rosemary/Sage followed the player character here, they won't go any farther east.

EXAMINE STUMP: Judging by the size of its stump, this tree must have been enormous. You see an axe embedded in the tree stump.

EXAMINE AXE: The axe is dulled from frequent use.

BEND IN THE ROAD exits are:

> EAST page 38 ACTION CASTLE
> SOUTH page 34 OLD POND ROAD

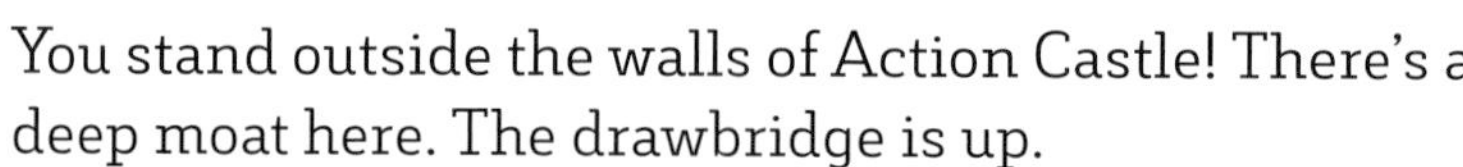

ACTION CASTLE

MENU

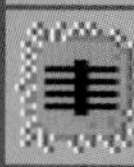

You stand outside the walls of Action Castle! There's a deep moat here. The drawbridge is up.

EXAMINE MOAT: The black, murky water ripples as something moves below its surface.

> If the player character doesn't have the sharpened axe and tries to ENTER MOAT:

As you enter the water, a monstrous catfish as big as a horse rears up and drags you away in its jaws. THE END.

> If the player character has the sharpened axe:

As you enter the water, a monstrous catfish as big as a horse rears up, but you manage to fend it off with your sharp axe. Wounded, it sinks once more below the surface of the murky water.

ACTION CASTLE exits are:
> WEST page 37 BEND IN THE ROAD
⚄ ENTER MOAT page 39

MOAT

You are treading water in the moat, just within reach of the castle's stone walls. You don't feel safe here.

EXAMINE WALLS: Peering closely, you notice a loose stone in the wall.

MOVE STONE: Pulling with all your might, you move the stone away, revealing a tunnel.

ENTER TUNNEL: You squeeze through the narrow opening and enter a long dark tunnel...

> Entering the tunnel leads Underground.

MOAT exits are:
> OUT page 38 ACTION CASTLE
⚄ ENTER TUNNEL page 39 UNDERGROUND

UNDERGROUND

You find yourself somewhere underneath the castle. A dark tunnel stretches to the north and south. There's a hole dug into the wall to the east. There is a skeleton here.

EXAMINE TUNNEL: To the north you see light filtering in from outside. To the south you hear a deep rumbling sound.

EXAMINE SKELETON: You see the skeletal remains of an adventurer clad in fire-scorched armor. Its rent and battered shield bears the heraldry of Action Castle!

UNDERGROUND exits are:
> NORTH page 39 MOAT
> SOUTH page 40 TREASURE TROVE
> EAST page 42 DUNGEON

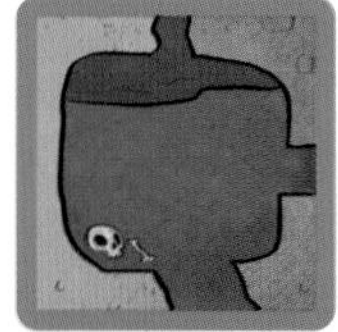

TREASURE TROVE

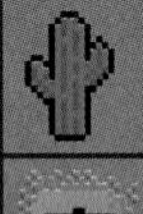

Eyes blinking, you emerge into a large chamber with a high, vaulted ceiling. A huge dragon is here, slumbering atop a pile of glittering treasure.

EXAMINE DRAGON: You see a huge beast with razor-sharp claws and a scaly hide stronger than steel. The dragon is lying on a mountain of treasure and snoring loudly.

EXAMINE TREASURE: You see burlap sacks bursting with gold coins, a king's ransom of precious gems, rings and jewelry and a gleaming sword forged of the finest steel.

EXAMINE GOLD: Stolen from the king's treasury, no doubt—you recognize the royal seal.

EXAMINE GEMS/RINGS/JEWELRY: You find an especially beautiful diamond ring. The gem is enormous!

EXAMINE SWORD: The sword isn't just gleaming... it's glowing!

> The dragon will wake and kill anyone who tries to steal from it. Any other move besides exiting the room will wake the dragon.

WAKE DRAGON: The dragon wakes up, eyes you hungrily and roars, "Another mortal dares challenge me? Choose a weapon: wits or steel."

CHOOSE STEEL: Even wearing the armor and shield, the player has no chance against the dragon. It knocks the shield aside, then breathes fire on the player. THE END.

CHOOSE WITS: "Excellent! Answer my riddle correctly or be burned alive and eaten! Are you ready?"

TREASURE TROVE exits are:

> NORTH page 39 UNDERGROUND

TREASURE TROVE (CONTINUED)

SAY YES: "Who owns nothing yet has everything?"

ANSWER "A WISE MAN/WOMAN": The dragon laughs. "Well done! You succeeded where all others failed. Now, choose your reward!" The dragon gestures to the gold coins, the gleaming sword and the diamond ring.

> If the player gives any other answer:

The dragon roars, "Wrong!" and breathes fire at you. THE END.

CHOOSE GOLD: The dragon laughs evilly. "Have you learned nothing? Well, take as much as you can carry!" he bellows. You grab a large sack of gold and stuff your pockets with any coins that spill out.

> Returning to the Moat with the gold coins is deadly:

You plunge into the murky water. Weighed down by the gold coins, you swiftly sink to the bottom of the moat and drown. THE END.

CHOOSE SWORD: "The sword of the fallen champion? A bold choice!" roars the dragon. "Now begone, and leave me to my slumber." You strap the sword to your waist, and the dragon goes back to sleep.

> Attacking the dragon is ill-advised, even with the sword:

The creature bats the sword aside and burns you alive with dragon fire. THE END.

CHOOSE RING: "A human who loves pretty rocks?" roars the dragon. "Typical!" With a sweep of its tail, the dragon opens a chute beneath your feet, and you tumble down into the darkness.

> The player character emerges from the Hermit's Cave (page 36). The hermit's fire still burns, but he's no longer there."

DUNGEON

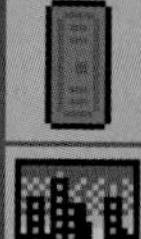

You are in the dungeon. Torches flicker high above, casting sinister shadows on the walls. A twisting staircase leads up. There are some cells here.

EXAMINE STAIRCASE: The stone staircase is lit by torches and leads upstairs.

TAKE TORCH: The torches are just out of reach.

EXAMINE CELL: You see a series of lines scratched into the wall. It looks like someone was here for a loooong time. There's a hole dug into one of the cell's walls.

EXAMINE HOLE: It's crude, probably made by a prisoner who attempted to escape.

> Entering the hole leads Underground.

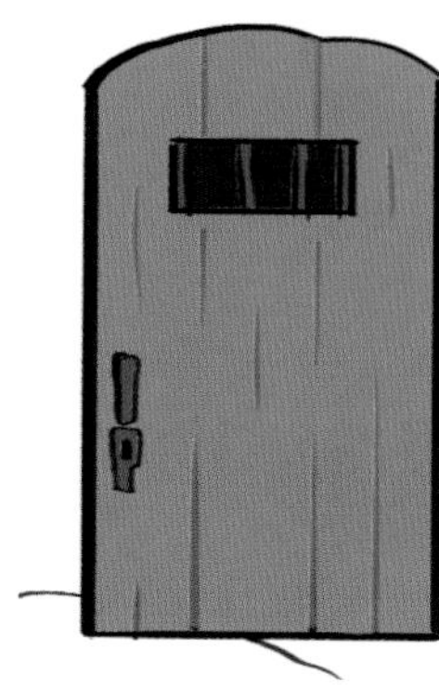

DUNGEON exits are:

> UP page 43 DUNGEON STAIRS

> HOLE page 39 UNDERGROUND

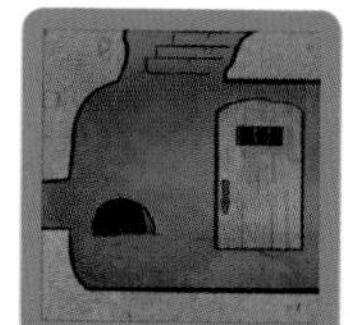

DUNGEON STAIRS

You are on the dungeon stairs. From above, you can make out some of the king's guards talking about current events. Someone's left an old lamp here.

LISTEN TO GUARDS: It seems the king's champion was slain by a terrible dragon and there's nobody left who is brave enough to venture underground.

EXAMINE LAMP: This old lamp seems like it's seen some use. It ran out of oil ages ago.

> The lamp cannot be lit. RUB LAMP also does nothing. It's pretty useless.

DUNGEON STAIRS exits are:

> UP page 44 COURTYARD

> DOWN page 42 DUNGEON

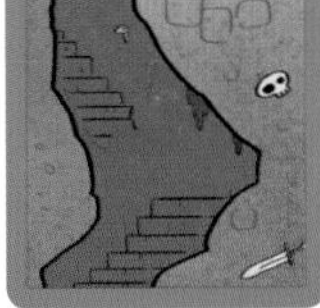

COURTYARD

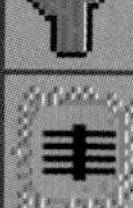

There is a pair of guards here. They yell, "Halt! Who goes there?"

> If the player character doesn't have the sword:

The guards grab you by the arms. You are arrested for trespassing and locked in the dungeon. This is where you remain for the rest of your miserable days. THE END.

> If the player character has the sword:

The guards grab you by the arms. One notices your sword and says, "Wait! The king will want to see this. Come with us." They escort you through a great hall to the throne room.

> The player character is taken to the Throne Room (page 45).

COURTYARD exits are:

> NONE

THRONE ROOM

You are in the throne room of Action Castle. The king is here. He sits upon an ornate gold throne. A pair of royal guards waits by the door.

GO WEST: The royal guards block your path.

EXAMINE KING: The king has a long, flowing beard and wears a gold crown.

> If the player character gave the slippers to the hermit, the king is wearing them!

ASK KING ABOUT SLIPPERS: "Quite well made!" He winks.

GIVE SWORD TO KING: "This kingdom needs a clever mind as much as it needs a keen blade. And as I'm in need of a new champion, I offer the position to you! Do you accept?"

SAY YES: The king touches your shoulder with the flat of the sword's blade and pronounces you the new champion of Action Castle! THE END.

SAY NO: The king sighs with great sadness. "Ah, then perhaps you are not the One." The royal guards escort you back to the town square, and you return to your simple life as a cobbler. But maybe, one day, you will return to Action Castle! THE END.

INVENTORY CHECKLIST

These items may be carried by the player:

- [x] Penny
- [ ] Slippers
- [ ] Blanket
- [ ] Axe
- [ ] Armor
- [ ] Shield
- [ ] Gold
- [ ] Ring
- [ ] Sword
- [ ] Lamp

SCORING

The player can earn a maximum of 100 points:

Each location visited . . . .+2 (total of 32 points)

Making a wish in the wishing well . . . .+3

Giving the blanket to Rosemary/Sage. . . . .+10

Giving the slippers to the hermit . . . .+10

Defeating the monster catfish . . . .+10

Answering the dragon's riddle . . . .+10

Becoming the king's champion . . . . +20

Proposing to Rosemary/Sage. . . . . +20

Finishing without saving . . . .+5

It all comes down to this.

Beneath Action Castle

Centuries since its fall, explore the ruins of Action Castle and delve beneath its halls with a party of brave adventurers this epic quest of good versus evil!

CONTENT RATED BY MMTRB

FANTASY

EXPERIENCED

EVERYONE (10+)

ACTION CASTLE III MAP

DARK FOREST

BANDIT CAMP

CROSSROADS

CAVE ENTRANCE

FISSURE

DARK CAVERN

MUSHROOM GARDEN

SPIDER LAIR

DEEP RAVINE

THRONE ROOM

GOBLIN CAVES

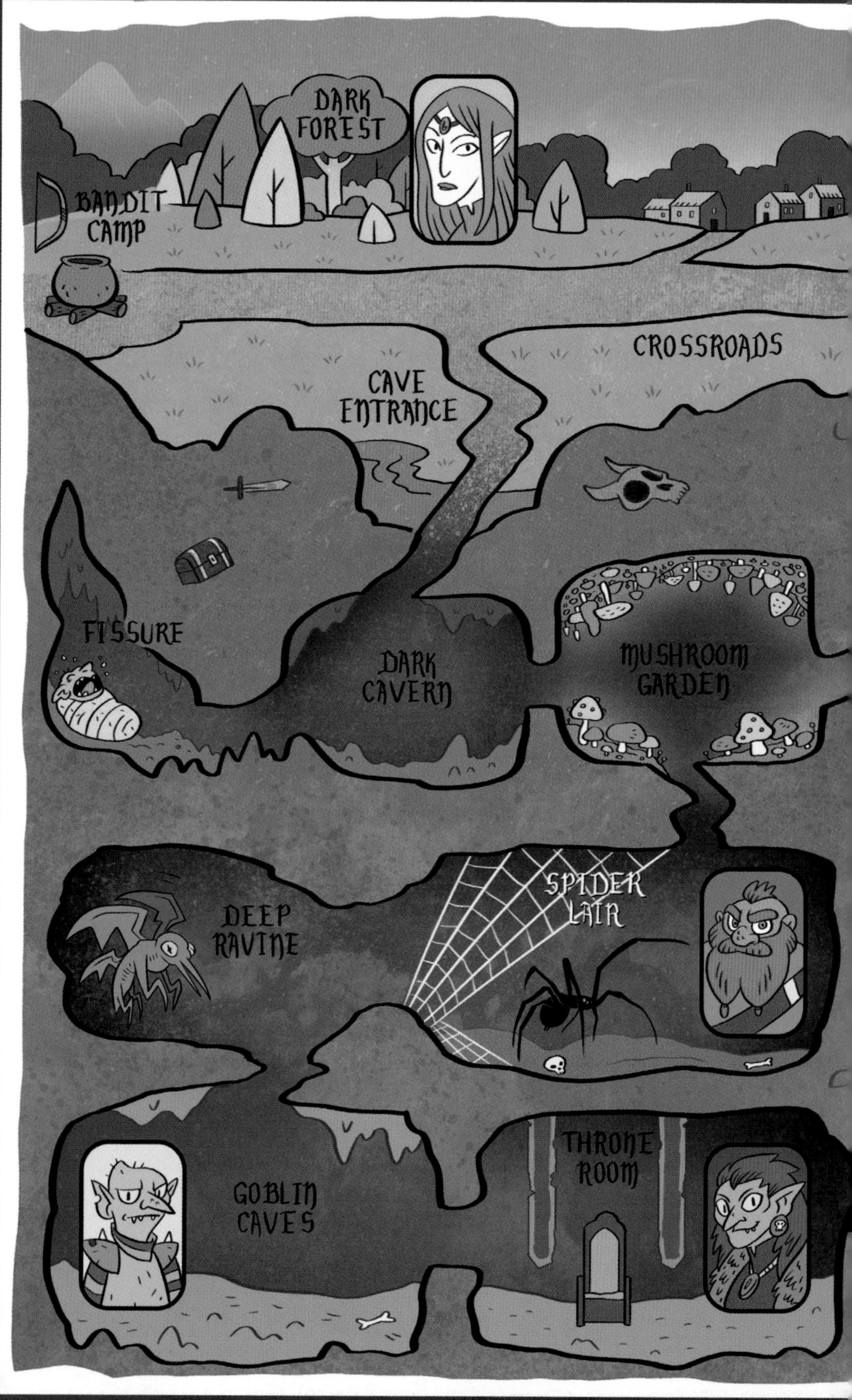

WIZARD
TOWER
RUINS
VAULT
DUNGEON
DARK
CORRIDOR
TORTURE
CHAMBER
SANCTUM
CHAOS
CHAPEL
CRYPT

CROSSROADS

You stand at a crossroads. The ruins of the once-glorious Action Castle lie to the east. A dark forest looms to the west. The road north will take you home.

> The player character starts with a backpack, which contains a lantern, a dagger, lockpicks and a waterskin.

GO NORTH: Are you sure you want to return home and end your adventure?

> If the player confirms, refer to the Epilogues section (page 72).

CROSSROADS exits are:
☒ NORTH page 72 EPILOGUES
> EAST page 62 CASTLE RUINS
> WEST page 51 DARK FOREST

DARK FOREST

You stand at the edge of a dark forest. Smoke rises to the west. A trail leads south. Through the trees you spy a shadowy figure watching your every move.

EXAMINE/TALK TO SHADOWY FIGURE: The figure steps out of the shadows. "Good, you're not one of them." You can make out the delicate features and pointed ears of an elf.

EXAMINE ELF: She wears a green cloak and carries a quiver of arrows.

TALK TO ELF: "A group of bandits ambushed me while I was exploring the ruins. There were too many to fight, so I ran into the forest. I dropped my bow during my escape."

INVITE ELF: The elf clasps your wrist. "Together, nothing can stop us!"

DARK FOREST exits are:

> SOUTH page 53 CAVERN ENTRANCE

> EAST page 50 CROSSROADS

> WEST page 52 BANDIT CAMP

BANDIT CAMP

Through the trees you spy a clearing where a group of bandits has made camp.

> If the player character brings the crying goblin baby here, it will alert the bandits. The player must then try to FIGHT BANDITS or CAST SLEEP.

EXAMINE BANDITS: You see a group of bandits gathered around a campfire. Above the fire hangs a stew pot. One of the bandits is admiring a fine bow.

EXAMINE POT: It's empty now, but you could cook a meal if you had ingredients.

> A player can make mushroom stew using spring water and cave mushrooms.

EXAMINE BOW: A fine elvish bow—strong, supple and light as a feather.

FIGHT BANDITS: The bandits are more than enough to handle the likes of you. They loot what they can and drag you off into the woods to be eaten by wild animals. THE END.

> The player character cannot beat the bandits in a fight; a player must CAST SLEEP on them to retrieve the bow.

BANDIT CAMP exits are:

> EAST page 51 DARK FOREST

CAVERN ENTRANCE

You come across an outcrop of mossy boulders. A gap between the rocks appears to lead down into the darkness. A natural spring bubbles up from the ground nearby.

EXAMINE SPRING: The water looks clean and clear, but looks can be deceiving.

ASK ELF ABOUT SPRING: She tells you that the water is safe to drink.

FILL WATERSKIN: You replenish your water supply.

ENTER CAVERN: It's too dark to see!

> A player must LIGHT LANTERN first. When the lantern is lit, the player character may enter the Dark Cavern.

ENTER CAVERN: You crawl inside the dark cavern and descend a steep slope.

CAVERN ENTRANCE exits are:

> NORTH page 51 DARK FOREST

⊠ ENTER CAVERN 54 DARK CAVERN

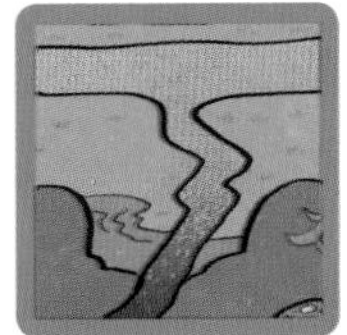

DARK CAVERN

You emerge into a large cavern. A steep slope leads back to the surface. To the east is a cramped passage. You hear soft mewling cries from within a crack in the wall.

EXAMINE WALL: You think you could squeeze inside the fissure if you weren't wearing your pack.

> A player must drop the backpack in order to enter the fissure.

DARK CAVERN exits are:

> EAST page 56 MUSHROOM GARDEN
> UP page 53 CAVERN ENTRANCE
⊠ ENTER FISSURE page 55 FISSURE

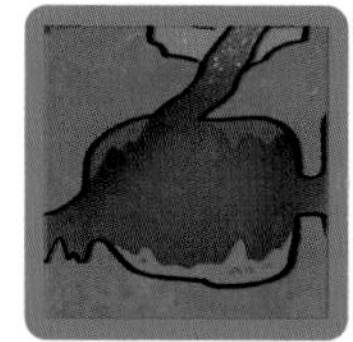

FISSURE

You're barely able to squeeze in. Wedged deep inside is a bundle wrapped in rags.

TAKE BUNDLE: As you reach down for the bundle, it squirms and lets out a shriek, and you recoil in surprise!

EXAMINE BUNDLE: You see a wrinkly face with green skin, yellow catlike eyes and a tuft of red hair. It's a baby goblin, probably abandoned.

TAKE BABY: The hungry baby shrieks and cries when you pick it up.

> The baby will cry whenever a player enters a new location. Feeding it some mushroom stew will sate its hunger and cause it to fall asleep. It will not eat or drink anything else.

DROP BABY: Being a parent is an awesome responsibility. You can't just abandon the little guy.

> The player character is stuck with the baby.

FISSURE exits are:

> OUT page 54 DARK CAVERN

MUSHROOM GARDEN

MENU

You are in a wide chamber carpeted with purple-spotted cave mushrooms. To the south is a narrow tunnel choked with cobwebs. A cramped passage leads west.

EXAMINE MUSHROOMS: The purple-spotted mushrooms are carefully laid out in rows.

ASK ELF ABOUT MUSHROOMS: They may taste bad to us, but the goblin tribes harvest these mushrooms for food.

TAKE MUSHROOM: You break off a chunk of a cave mushroom and stuff it into your pack.

> If the player arrived from the slide trap in the Vault, the mushrooms are smashed:

EXAMINE MUSHROOMS: Chunks of smashed mushroom are scattered across the floor.

TAKE MUSHROOM: You pick up a fist-sized hunk of cave mushroom and stuff it into your pack.

> You cannot climb the steep chute.

MUSHROOM GARDEN exits are:

> SOUTH page 57 SPIDER LAIR
> WEST page 54 DARK CAVERN

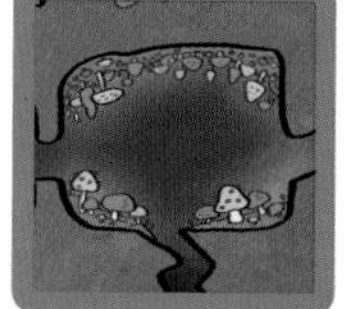

SPIDER LAIR

The tunnel ends in a large web that spans the western exit. Beyond is a sheer drop-off. A narrow tunnel leads north. A pair of bodies hangs from the ceiling.

EXAMINE WEB: You see a spiderweb that blocks the passage to the west. You are alarmed to find a large wolf spider sitting in the center, venom dripping from its fangs.

EXAMINE SPIDER: It's the size of a small horse. It's nearly camouflaged against the rock.

EXAMINE BODIES: You see a desiccated goblin corpse and a freshly caught dwarf wrapped in strands of spider silk. As you approach, the dwarf struggles weakly in his bonds.

> If a player walks west into the web, damages the web or attempts to free the dwarf while the spider is present, it will attack the player character:

The spider pounces on you and sinks its fangs into your body. Paralyzed, you watch helplessly as you're wrapped up in a cocoon and hung from the ceiling. THE END.

> If the elf has her bow, she can SHOOT SPIDER:

The elf draws back her bow and fires an arrow deep into the spider's abdomen. The creature hisses and retreats through the western exit.

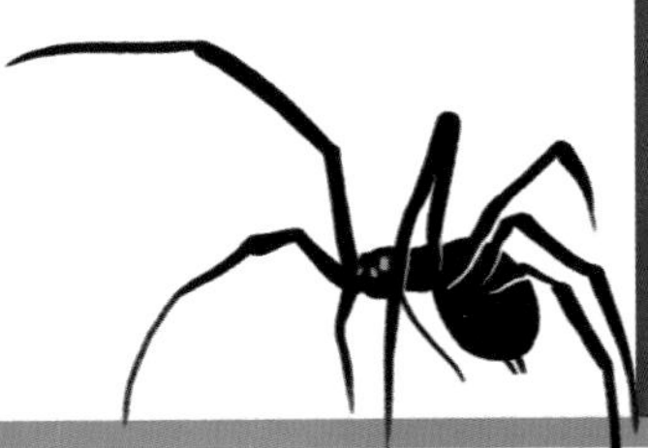

SPIDER LAIR exits are:

> NORTH page 56 MUSHROOM GARDEN
⊠ WEST page 59 DEEP RAVINE

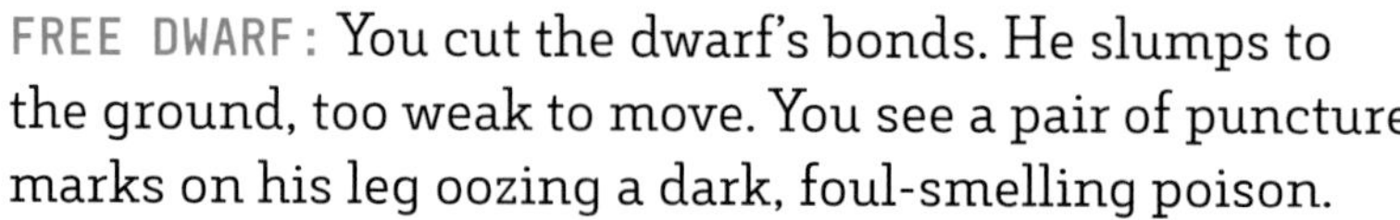

SPIDER LAIR (CONTINUED)

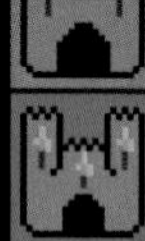

FREE DWARF: You cut the dwarf's bonds. He slumps to the ground, too weak to move. You see a pair of puncture marks on his leg oozing a dark, foul-smelling poison.

> If the cleric has joined the party, he may HEAL DWARF: The cleric utters a prayer and the poisoned bite is healed. The dwarf cannot join the party while poisoned.

EXAMINE DWARF: A short, stout bearded fellow. He carries a hatchet and pickaxe.

TALK TO DWARF: "I was searching for gold and gems when the spider ambushed me!"

INVITE DWARF: The dwarf hefts his pickaxe. "Aye, let's go bash some heads!"

> Webs block the western exit; the dwarf can USE HATCHET to clear a path.

DEEP RAVINE

Steps carved into the rock lead down from the eastern tunnel into a deep ravine. A flock of leathery-winged creatures is affixed to the body of a large spider on which they're feeding.

> If the player character brings the crying goblin baby here, it will alert the stirges:

The baby's wailing alerts the creatures to your presence. They swarm you, stabbing at you with their beaks and draining you of your precious bodily fluids. THE END.

> If the baby goblin was fed, it remains quiet and the party can sneak past the stirges without incident.

EXAMINE SPIDER: It's quite dead. An arrow protrudes from its bulbous body. It's currently swarming with cat-sized birdlike things.

EXAMINE THINGS: A loathsome combination of bat, bird and mosquito. The creatures are feeding on the spider's corpse with their sharp, needle-like beaks.

The dwarf will identify the creatures as bloodsucking stirges.

DEEP RAVINE exits are:

> EAST page 57 SPIDER LAIR

⊠ DOWN page 60 GOBLIN CAVES

GOBLIN CAVES

MENU

You walk the length of the ravine and soon enter a maze of twisting passages. The dwarf guides you through a network of tunnels, switchbacks and flooded grottoes. He stops, sniffs the air and warns, "Beware! There be goblins about."

GO {anywhere}: As if on cue, a large net drops from the ceiling, ensnaring the party. Goblins emerge from the tunnels and surround you. They brandish spears and yell threats.

> If the player doesn't have the baby:

The goblins enslave you and your allies, and you're forced to spend the rest of your miserable lives turning big rocks into little rocks. THE END.

SHOW BABY: The goblins whisper to one another, and you are freed from the net. One of them prods you toward the eastern exit with a spear.

GO NORTH: The goblins poke at you with their spears, suggesting you travel east.

GO EAST: The goblins escort you into a squalid chamber filled with treasure.

> The player character is taken to the Throne Room (page 61). Upon subsequent visits, the player is free to travel east or back to the north.

GOBLIN CAVES exits are:

> NORTH page 59 DEEP RAVINE
⊡ EAST page 61 THRONE ROOM

THRONE ROOM

Balanced on top of a pile of treasure is an ornate gold throne. On it sits a diminutive goblin dressed in furs, feathers and jewelry looted from the castle's vault.

EXAMINE GOBLIN: The goblin queen! She has yellow, catlike eyes and wild red hair.

> The player character must give the baby to the queen to be allowed to leave.

GIVE BABY: The goblin queen showers the baby with kisses and coos lovingly at it.

> She will allow the player character to leave unless they carry the gold crown, in which case she wants a gift!

TALK TO QUEEN: The goblin queen shrieks, "Tribute!"

> If the player character has the crown, it may be traded with the goblin queen:

GIVE CROWN: The goblin queen claps her hands with delight and places the crown on her head. She rummages through her treasures and throws a tarnished artifact at your feet.

THRONE ROOM exits are:

⊠ WEST page 60 GOBLIN CAVES

MENU

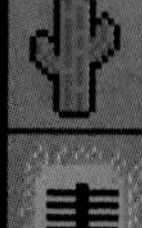

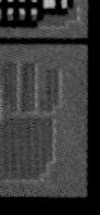

THRONE ROOM (CONTINUED)

EXAMINE ARTIFACT: It's a hammered bronze javelin shaped like a lightning bolt.

> Once the audience with the queen is over, the player character is escorted back to the surface.

The goblins march you out of the room and escort you through the dangerous caverns to the cavern entrance.

> The player character returns to the Cavern Entrance (page 53).

CASTLE RUINS

All that's left of Action Castle is this courtyard, a lonely tower and a few crumbling walls. A rickety wooden stairway leads up to the tower. A dark stairwell descends to the dungeon.

GO DOWN: It's too dark to see!

> A player must LIGHT LANTERN in order for the player character to continue down the dark stairwell.

CASTLE RUINS exits are:

> WEST page 50 CROSSROADS

> UP page 63 WIZARD'S TOWER

☒ DOWN page 64 DUNGEON

WIZARD'S TOWER

You enter the tower to find it cluttered with old books. There's a wizard here, peering through a telescope.

EXAMINE BOOKS: You spy a dizzying array of occult tomes in a variety of languages. One of the few you can understand is a journal entitled *Ecology of the Ooze.*

READ JOURNAL: "...the gray ooze in particular prefers a warm, dark environment where it can ambush the unwary by dropping down from above. It then engulfs and digests its prey..."

EXAMINE WIZARD: An old man with a long beard and blue robes adorned with moons and stars. He holds a wand.

EXAMINE WAND: The wand looks as if it were carved from a piece of ice. It's covered in runes. One rune still glows with dim blue light, while the others are dull and faded.

ATTACK WIZARD: The wizard brandishes his wand and blasts you with a ray of frost. You are frozen solid. THE END.

TALK TO WIZARD: "Have you come across a spell book in your travels? I seem to have misplaced mine!"

USE TELESCOPE: You look through the telescope and see the twinkling stars of the night sky. The wizard grabs your arm and says, "The Great Dragon is aligned with the Celestial Goat! Something dark and terrible draws near, and only we can stop it!"

INVITE WIZARD: He puts on his hat. "May the stars guide us!"

WIZARD'S TOWER exits are:

> DOWN page 62 CASTLE RUINS

DUNGEON

MENU

You enter the dungeon. A dark corridor runs east to west. A stone stair leads up. There are a few dark and dingy cells here.

EXAMINE CELLS: The dirty cells are empty save for straw bedding strewn about.

SEARCH: You search the cells and find a shiny pendant buried under the straw bedding.

EXAMINE PENDANT: It's some kind of holy symbol shaped like a fist holding a lightning bolt. The metal is cheap pewter worth only a few copper pieces.

DUNGEON exits are:
> WEST page 65 VAULT
> EAST page 66 DARK CORRIDOR
> UP page 62 CASTLE RUINS

VAULT

You enter a vaulted chamber filled with broken crates and empty shelves. If anything valuable was here, it was looted a long time ago. There's a large stone statue here.

EXAMINE STATUE: This large stone statue depicts a stern-looking figure clad in armor. Its fist is raised to the heavens and has suffered some damage.

> A player cannot repair the damaged statue.

EXAMINE FIST: Some of its fingers are broken off, as if something was pried loose.

> If the cleric has joined the party:

ASK CLERIC ABOUT STATUE: "It's the Lord of Law and Justice, though he's usually depicted holding a bronze javelin."

> Tampering with the statue (pushing, pulling, etc.) causes a slide trap to suddenly open in the floor:

A trapdoor opens beneath your feet, sending you tumbling down a steep chute to a cavern below. You land in a sprawling heap atop a cluster of cave mushrooms. Miraculously, they break your fall. You suffer only minor bruises.

The player character arrives in the Mushroom Garden (page 56).

> Once the trap is sprung, it will remain open and visible.

VAULT exits are:

> EAST page 64 DUNGEON

DARK CORRIDOR

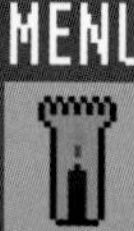

You're walking down a long, dark corridor. At the far end is an iron door covered in spikes. There are some human remains here.

EXAMINE REMAINS: You see a gruesome sight: a pair of severed arms clutching a small metal lockbox. The rest of the body is nowhere to be found; apart from the arms, only an iron belt buckle and half a leather boot remain. The stone underneath is stained and corroded.

> An ooze lurks above, waiting to devour another unfortunate victim. Taking the lockbox or picking the lock causes the ooze to drop down and engulf the player character, who is slowly and painfully digested:

Something slimy and wet drops down from the ceiling and engulfs you in corrosive gray slime. You try to scream, but no sound comes out as you are slowly dissolved and digested. THE END.

LOOK CEILING/LOOK UP: Looking up, you see an undulating mass of translucent gray protoplasm clinging to the ceiling, almost invisible in the flickering light from the lantern.

USE WAND ON OOZE: The gray blob freezes solid, falls to the floor and shatters.

TAKE BELT BUCKLE/LEATHER BOOT: Junk. You don't need this.

EXAMINE LOCKBOX: It's a box. It's locked. It's a lockbox.

DARK CORRIDOR exits are:
☒ EAST page 68 TORTURE CHAMBER
> WEST page 64 DUNGEON

DARK CORRIDOR (CONTINUED)

PICK LOCK: It takes time, but you manage to pick the lock. Inside is a crown.

EXAMINE CROWN: It must have belonged to the ruler of Action Castle. It's solid gold and encrusted with gems and fit for a king... or a queen.

GO EAST: The door is closed.

EXAMINE SPIKED DOOR: The massive door is covered in rust. It doesn't appear to be locked.

OPEN DOOR: The door makes an awful screech as you wrench it open.

> Fortunately, nothing else happens. The noise is just to scare the players.

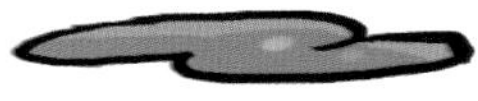

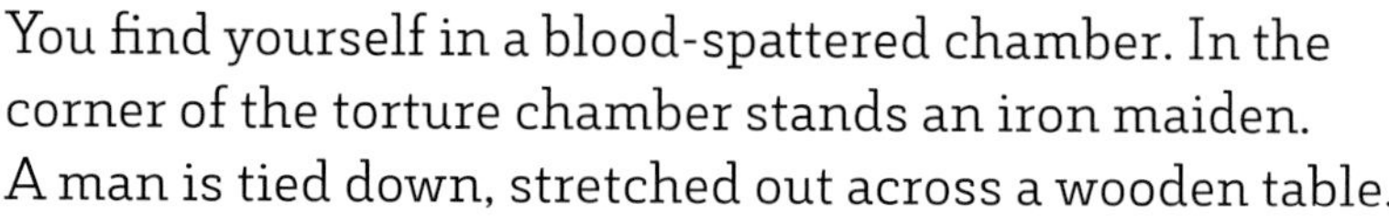

MENU
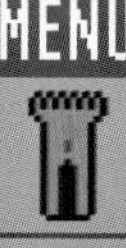

You find yourself in a blood-spattered chamber. In the corner of the torture chamber stands an iron maiden. A man is tied down, stretched out across a wooden table.

EXAMINE IRON MAIDEN: The rusting metal sarcophagus is cast in the shape of a young woman.

OPEN IRON MAIDEN: The front of the maiden swings open, revealing a spiked interior... and a descending spiral staircase.

EXAMINE MAN: He's tied to the table at the wrists and ankles. He shows signs of torture, but he is still alive. His tabard is emblazoned with the sigil of a lightning bolt.

TALK TO MAN: He croaks, "Water..."

> If the man is given water and released from his bonds:

The cleric invokes a prayer—"By the Power of the Light..."—and his wounds are magically healed.

INVITE CLERIC: "By the Light, we shall defeat the forces of Chaos!"

GIVE PENDANT TO CLERIC: "Thank you! With this I can destroy any undead creature that plagues the land of the living."

> He can USE PENDANT to destroy the skeletal warriors in the Crypt. He can also INVOKE PRAYER or CAST HEAL to cure the poisoned dwarf in the Spider Lair.

TORTURE CHAMBER exits are:

> WEST page 66 DARK CORRIDOR

⊡ DOWN page 69 SANCTUM

SANCTUM

You are in the inner sanctum of a hidden temple. A large tome rests on a lectern. Set within an alcove is a spiral staircase leading up. You smell burning incense to the west.

> If the player character has the bronze javelin:

You hear ominous chanting from the chamber to the west.

EXAMINE TOME: The large, leather-bound book is opened to an illustration of an armored man throwing a lightning bolt at a massive horned demon.

TAKE TOME: It's too large to carry.

ASK CLERIC ABOUT TOME: The cleric exclaims, "Ah, the eternal struggle between Good and Evil, Law and Chaos!"

SANCTUM exits are:

> WEST page 70 CHAOS CHAPEL
> UP page 68 TORTURE CHAMBER

CHAOS CHAPEL

MENU

The chapel is lit by flickering oil lamps, and the air is heavy with incense. In the center of the chamber is a large pit ringed with spikes. To the south is the crypt.

EXAMINE PIT: It's deep and dark; you cannot see the bottom.

> If the player character is carrying the bronze javelin, the Chaos cultist will be here:

A black-robed man is here, chanting in some foul tongue. He utters a terrible word of power and a gout of green flame erupts from the pit! When the smoke clears, you see a monstrous demon clawing its way up from the pit's infernal depths.

EXAMINE DEMON: The demon is horned and tusked. It is covered in writhing tentacles and stands at least 12 feet tall.

THROW JAVELIN AT DEMON: The javelin transforms into a bolt of pure energy and pierces the demon's heart. You hear a crack of thunder, and your senses are dazzled by a burst of white light. When you recover, the demon is gone!

> Any other action or attempt to flee results in a grisly demise. THE END.

> Once the demon is defeated, only the Chaos cultist remains:

The cultist sneers, "You fool! Do you think you've won? You've only delayed the inevitable! When the stars are right, the Dark One will rise once more!" He begins chanting, and the room darkens...

> A player can now defeat the cultist by pushing him into the pit.

CHAOS CHAPEL exits are:

> SOUTH page 71 CRYPT

> EAST page 69 SANCTUM

CRYPT

This long, narrow chamber is artfully adorned with skulls and bones. Many skeletal bodies are entombed here, still clad in their mouldering armor.

EXAMINE SKELETAL BODIES: One of the skeletons grips a spell book in its bony hands.

TAKE BOOK: The skeletal warriors rise from their eternal sleep, weapons drawn and clawed fingers outstretched.

> If the cleric is absent or the pendant hasn't been recovered, the player is doomed:

They close in, and you soon join their unholy ranks! THE END.

> If the cleric is here and has the pendant, he can use it to destroy the undead:

TURN UNDEAD/USE PENDANT: A flash of light from the pendant turns the skeletal warriors to ash.

EXAMINE SPELL BOOK: It's covered in cosmological symbols. The contents are indecipherable.

ASK ELF ABOUT SPELLS: "I recognize this—it's the Spell of Sleep. Alas, I have not learned how to wield such magic."

SHOW/GIVE SPELL BOOK TO WIZARD: "My spell book! I must have dropped it when I fled the crypt."

CRYPT exits are:

> NORTH page 70 CHAOS CHAPEL

EPILOGUES

When the player character returns home by going north from the crossroads, the game ends. Read one of these epilogues, based on the character's progress....

> If the player character made no real progress before returning home:

It seems that a life of adventure just isn't for you. You return to your village, grow old and die alone and unloved. THE END.

> If the player character returns home with the baby goblin:

You return to your village with the baby and raise it as your own. Many years later, inspired by your tales of adventure, the young goblin leaves home to explore the ruins of Action Castle. You never see him again, but one day you receive a letter in the mail—from Mipple, the Goblin Prince. You couldn't be more proud. THE END.

> If the player character returns home with the gold crown:

You end up selling the crown to an antiques dealer and make a small fortune, which you promptly and foolishly gamble away. THE END.

> If the player character returns home with the bronze javelin:

Your party journeys to the cleric's stronghold, where he returns the artifact. You are awarded a medal and certificate of heroism at a ceremony, after which there is a small but tasteful reception. Wine and cheese are served. THE END.

> If the player character returns home after banishing the demon but without defeating the Chaos cultist:

Weeks later, you find yourself gazing up at the stars and pondering the cultist's prophecy. When the stars are

EPILOGUES (CONTINUED)

right once more, will you dare journey beneath Action Castle again? THE END?

> If the player character banished the demon and defeated the Chaos cultist:

Word of your exploits travels far and wide across the land. You retire as a hero, celebrated by everyone you meet. Many years later, while drinking at the local tavern, you see a familiar group of adventurers: an elf, a dwarf, a cleric and a wizard. From behind them, a red-haired goblin warrior steps forward with a treasure map and asks, "Will you join us?" TO BE CONTINUED!

INVENTORY CHECKLIST

These items may be carried by the player:

- ☒ Backpack
  - ☒ Waterskin
  - ☒ Lockpicks
  - ☒ Dagger
  - ☒ Lantern
- ☐ Water
- ☐ Bow
- ☐ Baby goblin
- ☐ Mushroom
- ☐ Bronze javelin
- ☐ Journal
- ☐ Pendant
- ☐ Lockbox
- ☐ Crown
- ☐ Spell book

SCORING

The player can earn a maximum of 100 points:

Returning the elf's bow . . . . +5
Returning the wizard's spell book . . . . +5
Rescuing the cleric . . . . +10
Rescuing the dwarf . . . . +10
Defeating the gray ooze . . . . +10
Defeating the spider . . . . +10
Rescuing the baby goblin . . . . +5
Giving the baby goblin to the goblin queen . . . . +5
Giving the crown to the goblin queen . . . . +5
Banishing the Chaos demon . . . . +10
Killing the Chaos cultist . . . . +10
Returning home . . . . +10
Raising the baby goblin as your own . . . . +5
Returning the artifact to the stronghold . . . . +5
Finishing without saving . . . . +5

BLACKBOARD
JUNGLE
Can you find your homework and avoid detention, or are you doomed to a weekend of staring at the wall?
CONTENT RATED BY MMTRB
HIGH SCHOOL
BEGINNER
EVERYONE (10+)

BLACKBOARD JUNGLE MAP

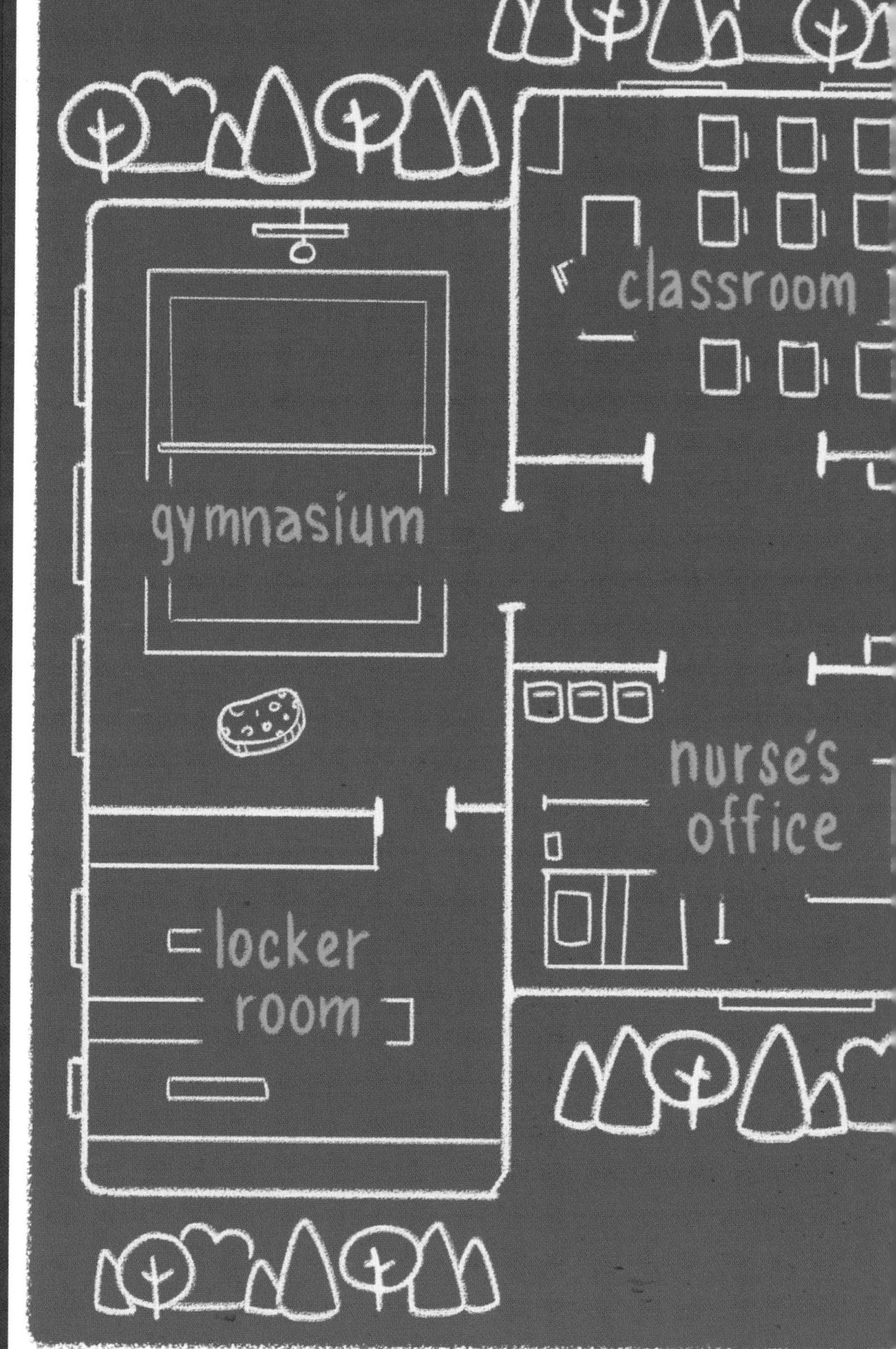

library
hallway
W
E

GYMNASIUM

You are in the gym. It's currently devoid of sweaty athletes and cheering fans. You smell a locker room to the south. The exit is to the east. You see an eyeglasses case on the ground.

EXAMINE CASE: Inside the case are a pair of cat-eye glasses.

EXAMINE GLASSES: The bedazzled cat-eye glasses aren't really your style.

WEAR GLASSES: Everything is blurry and indistinct.

> The player cannot see room contents, exits or examine objects while wearing the glasses.

GYMNASIUM exits are:

> SOUTH page 79 LOCKER ROOM
> EAST page 80 HALLWAY (WEST)

LOCKER ROOM

You are in one of Parsely High's locker rooms. There is a janitor's cart here.

EXAMINE CART: The janitor's cart is more or less a trash can on wheels. A bucket of pink sawdust and a broom hang from the cart.

> The player can push the cart around or take the individual items.

PUSH CART: You hear someone cry out in alarm from inside the cart's trash can.

EXAMINE TRASH CAN: You find a freshman.

TALK TO FRESHMAN: Are you serious? Someone might see you!

HELP FRESHMAN: The freshman runs off crying.

LOCKER ROOM exits are:
> NORTH page 78 GYMNASIUM

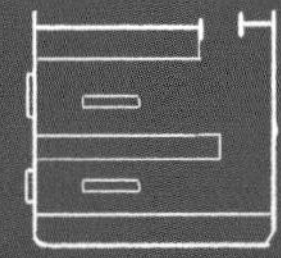

HALLWAY (WEST)

You're at the western end of a long hallway. Someone appears to have had tummy troubles; there's a puddle of sick on the floor. There's a classroom door here. The gym is to the west.

EXAMINE DOOR: You see Mr. Bushel discussing last night's homework. Oops.

EXAMINE PUDDLE OF SICK: Yuck. Looks like it was Salisbury steak day. Where's the school janitor when you need him?

> Going east without cleaning up the puddle causes the player character to slip and fall, sustaining a mild concussion.

You wake up in the nurse's office with a terrible headache and blurred vision. The school nurse sends you to the hospital for an MRI, just in case. THE END.

USE PINK SAWDUST: You cover up the slippery puddle.

> The Hallway is now safe. The player character may then proceed up the Hallway.

SWEEP: You'll make a fine janitor some day.

HALLWAY (WEST) exits are:

⊠ EAST page 81 HALLWAY (EAST)

> WEST page 78 GYMNASIUM

> NORTH page 83 CLASSROOM

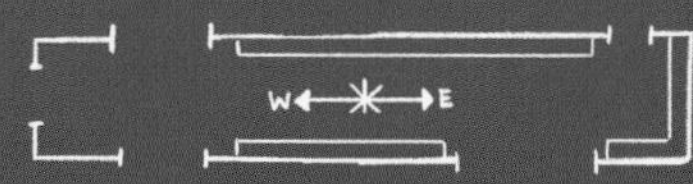

HALLWAY (EAST)

You stand at the eastern end of a long hallway. There are rows of lockers on either side of you. You see the door leading to the library.

EXAMINE LOCKERS: You find your locker. At least you think it's your locker. It's been a while since you opened it.

OPEN LOCKER: It's locked. There's a combination lock on it.

EXAMINE LOCK: The lock is your basic tempered steel, 32-digit combination lock. Very hard to crack! You've tried.

USE COMBINATION 16-32-64: The numbers on the lock don't go that high.

USE COMBINATION 8-16-32: The locker opens. There are some typewritten papers inside.

EXAMINE PAPERS: It's your English homework—something about something you were supposed to read. You paid good money for this!

HALLWAY (EAST) exits are:
⊠ NORTH page 82 LIBRARY
> WEST page 80 HALLWAY (WEST)

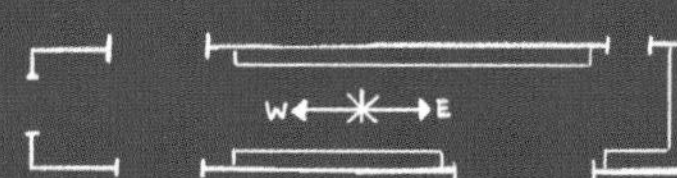

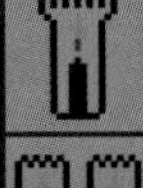

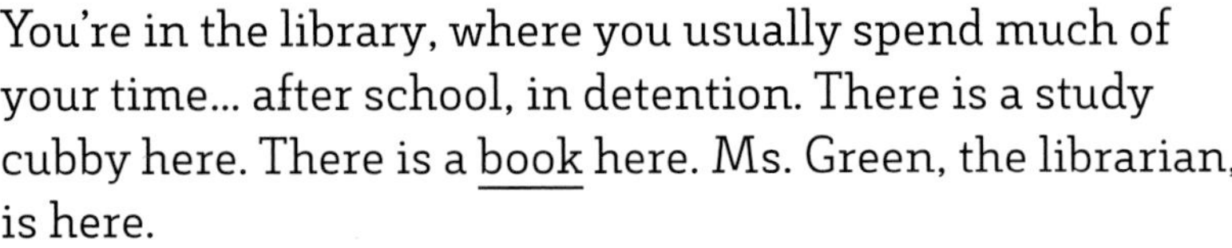

LIBRARY

You're in the library, where you usually spend much of your time... after school, in detention. There is a study cubby here. There is a book here. Ms. Green, the librarian, is here.

> If the player character never picked up the glasses or is sent to the Library a second time: You spend the next four hours staring at the wall. THE END.

GO OUT: The librarian blocks your path and squints at you. "You're here until the end of day!"

EXAMINE LIBRARIAN: She squints at you. She asks, "Back again, eh?"

EXAMINE BOOK: The book's title is *Cryptography for Dummies*. You remember skimming it during detention yesterday, but that seems like a long time ago.

READ BOOK: You flip it open. Someone wrote "Divide by two" in the margin of the book. Oh, that was you!

EXAMINE CUBBY: The wood desk has the numbers 16-32-64 scratched into it.

> This is the player's elaborate "code" for the combination. When divided by two, it reveals the correct combination: 8-16-32.

GIVE GLASSES TO LIBRARIAN: "Oh, thank you so much for these! I can't see a thing without them! Now, run along."

> If her glasses are returned, the librarian allows the player character to leave.

LIBRARY exits are:

⊠ SOUTH page 81 HALLWAY (EAST)

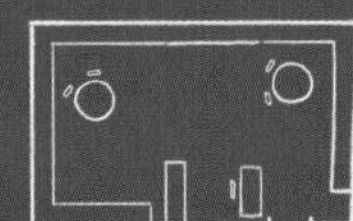

CLASSROOM

You step into the classroom, and your English teacher, Mr. Bushel, clears his throat. "Late as usual. I sincerely hope you remembered your homework." He holds out a hand.

If the player character doesn't have the English paper to turn in:

Mr. Bushel sends you off to the library for detention.

> The player arrives in the Library (page 82).

GIVE HOMEWORK TO MR. BUSHEL: "Well, well. Color me impressed!"

Your scheme seems to have worked out, allowing you to survive one more day in the Blackboard Jungle. THE END.

CLASSROOM exits are:

> NONE

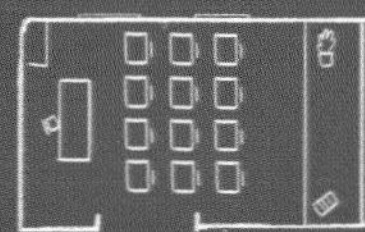

INVENTORY CHECKLIST

These items may be carried by the player:

- ☐ Eyeglasses case
- ☐ Cat-eye glasses
- ☐ Bucket
- ☐ Broom
- ☐ Homework
- ☐ Book

SCORING

The player can earn a maximum of 50 points:

Retrieving the cat-eye glasses . . . . +5
Sweeping up the hallway . . . . +1
Rescuing the freshman . . . . +1
Returning the cat-eye glasses . . . . +10
Unlocking your locker . . . . +10
...on the first try! . . . . +2
Handing in your English homework . . . . +20
Finishing without saving . . . . +1

DANGERTOWN
BEATDOWN
It's 1987, and Detective Jack Slade and his partner Jetta Chang must take down a crime boss and restore law and order.
CONTENT RATED BY MMTRB
ACTION
ADVANCED
MATURE (16+)

DANGERTOWN BEATDOWN MAP

MENU

GASLIGHT DISTRICT
NORTH END
ARCADE
STRIP CLUB
SOUTHSIDE
APARTMENT
DOWNTOWN
POLICE STATION

MENU

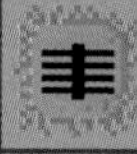

BEDROOM

You're roused from sleep by neon light streaming in through your window. It's 11:58 p.m.—time to start your day. There's a closet and a mirror here. Your answering machine is flashing. A door leads out.

EXAMINE MIRROR: You fell asleep wearing your clothes from yesterday: black jeans and a T-shirt that reads "Gheorghe's Gym—Little Italy." You're in good shape, but coffee is required.

EXAMINE WINDOW: A neon sign blinks on and off from the strip club across the street. Your motorcycle is parked where you left it.

EXAMINE SIGN: "TIGER'z DEN" blinks below a neon tiger.

EXAMINE ANSWERING MACHINE: The PLAY MESSAGE button is flashing.

PLAY MESSAGE: A voice says, "Slade, you're gonna pay for shutting down our operation. We have your partner. Bring us the tape. Come alone."

OPEN CLOSET: You see a police dress uniform and a leather jacket.

EXAMINE UNIFORM: The brass nameplate reads "J. SLADE."

WEAR UNIFORM: You wear your dress blues only for commendations and funerals.

WEAR JACKET: You put on the leather jacket. Your keys jingle in the pocket.

EXAMINE KEYS: These are the keys to your apartment and motorcycle.

BEDROOM exits are:

> OUT page 89 APARTMENT

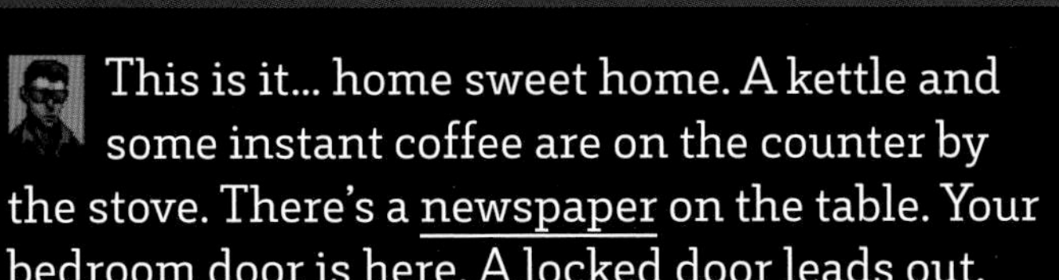

APARTMENT

This is it... home sweet home. A kettle and some instant coffee are on the counter by the stove. There's a newspaper on the table. Your bedroom door is here. A locked door leads out.

MAKE COFFEE: You perform the sacred ritual. You fill the kettle, set it down on the stove top to boil and wait.

READ NEWSPAPER: Violent crime is up eight percent in Santa Morena. Record-setting high temperatures are expected. The mayor is trying to pass another waterfront development deal, and some masked weirdo is beating up muggers and purse snatchers.

> Once the player character has made coffee and read the newspaper's headlines:

Someone knocks at the door and says, "Slade. Open up."

EXAMINE DOOR: The door is locked. You see a peephole.

EXAMINE PEEPHOLE or LOOK OUT: You spy a large man in a suit holding a baseball bat in his meaty fist. He raps hard on the door. "Open up. Let's talk."

> If the player doesn't comply:

He kicks in the door and enters—blocking the exit.

TALK TO MAN: "Boss D says it's time for you to take a little vacation. Maybe a drive up the coast. You come back in a month or two, all refreshed and ready to cooperate." He places an envelope on the table. "Consider this an advance to cover gas and tolls."

EXAMINE ENVELOPE: That's a lot of cash just for gas and tolls—about six months' pay.

TAKE ENVELOPE/CASH: Are you sure?

SAY YES: You feel sick to your stomach as you pocket the cash. Is this how you thought you'd end up, just another cop on the take? This is why the bad guys always win. THE END.

APARTMENT (CONTINUED)

MENU

SAY NO: "I figured you might turn us down, considering how well you're doing." He glances around your tiny apartment and shoulders the baseball bat, growling, "Well, since the carrot ain't working for you, let's try the stick." The kettle starts whistling...

HIT MAN WITH KETTLE: You grab the hot kettle and smash it into the gangster's skull. He collapses, dropping the baseball bat.

HIT MAN WITH BAT: He's already knocked out. You may be suspended, but you're still a good cop.

> If the player doesn't knock out the gangster:

The gangster bashes you to a bloody pulp. THE END.

SEARCH MAN: You search his pockets and find an empty matchbook and a wallet.

EXAMINE MATCHBOOK: There's a snarling tiger logo above the name "TIGER'z DEN."

EXAMINE WALLET: It contains a $100 bill and a California driver's license.

> A player can either remove the items or keep them inside the wallet.

EXAMINE LICENSE: The well-dressed thug's name is Rocco Falcone.

TAKE ENVELOPE: It's tempting, but it's blood money. When this goon wakes up, he'll take it back to his boss, which will send a clear message: you can't be bought.

GO OUT: You lock your door and head downstairs to the streets of Southside.

APARTMENT exits are:
> ENTER BEDROOM page 88
> OUT page 91 SOUTHSIDE

SOUTHSIDE

You're outside a rundown apartment building. There is a strip club here. How quaint—just like a Norman Rockwell painting. Gaslight's north end is just a short walk from here.

Your motorcycle is parked here.

EXAMINE MOTORCYCLE: A black Kawasaki GPZ900R. You call it "Baby."

GET ON MOTORCYCLE: You climb onto your bike.

> The first time the player character gets on, they must start up the bike using their keys.

> While on the bike, the player can DRIVE or RIDE to a new area of the map, as noted in the description. PARK BIKE or GET OFF BIKE will allow a player to leave the motorcycle and travel on foot. The player character cannot enter a location while on the bike.

> When the player character gets on the motorcycle, go to the Gaslight District (page 92).

SOUTHSIDE exits are:
> RIDE TO GASLIGHT DISTRICT page 92
> NORTH page 94 NORTH END
> ENTER APARTMENT page 89
> ENTER STRIP CLUB page 93

GASLIGHT DISTRICT

You're in Santa Morena's red-light district, where life is cheap but the rent ain't. If you're going to park your ride, best do it here in Southside. The gangbangers who rule Gaslight's North End would just love to take it off your hands.

PARK BIKE: You park your ride and hit the mean streets of Southside.

> The player character enters Southside (page 91).

GASLIGHT DISTRICT exits are:

> DRIVE/RIDE TO DOWNTOWN page 100

> DRIVE/RIDE TO LITTLE ITALY page 97

STRIP CLUB

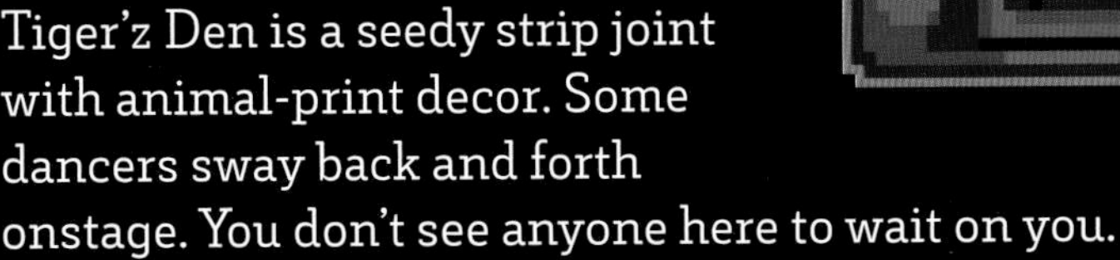

Tiger'z Den is a seedy strip joint with animal-print decor. Some dancers sway back and forth onstage. You don't see anyone here to wait on you.

EXAMINE DANCERS: Occasionally someone tips them a buck or two. They feign interest for a few seconds, then move on to the next customer.

TALK TO DANCERS: The dancers ignore you, focusing instead on the paying customers.

TIP DANCERS: A dancer slips the $100 bill into her G-string. Like magic, the club's lone waitress appears.

EXAMINE WAITRESS: It's your ex, Cat Marco. She doesn't look happy to see you.

TALK TO CAT: "Hi, Jack. Big spender! Did you finally bet on the right horse down at the racetrack?"

SHOW LICENSE TO CAT or ASK CAT ABOUT ROCCO: She replies, "Yeah, I know him. Gets a little too hands-on with the staff, but he works for Boss D, so nobody's got the guts to throw him out."

ASK CAT ABOUT BOSS D: She says, "He hired some girls for a party at his place. I hear some major players will be there—bankers, lawyers, politicians. I have an address. Got something to write on?"

GIVE MATCHBOOK TO CAT: She writes down an address: "Pacific Towers, Morena Beach."

> Cat will also tell the player character the address if they left the matchbook behind.

STRIP CLUB exits are:

> OUT page 91 SOUTHSIDE

MENU

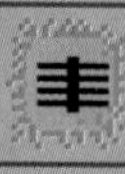

NORTH END

Welcome to Gaslight's picturesque North End, where you might find things that aren't on fire. Some gang members loiter outside an arcade. A pay phone is on the corner. Southside is a short walk from here.

EXAMINE GANG MEMBERS: They toss their cigarettes and head inside when they see you.

EXAMINE PAY PHONE: There's a quarter in the change slot.

USE PHONE: It's 25 cents to make a call.

USE QUARTER ON PHONE: No dial tone. Must be out of order. You hear the coin drop down into the change slot.

EXAMINE ARCADE: The arcade is neutral ground for the gangs of the Gaslight District.

NORTH END exits are:
> SOUTH page 91 SOUTHSIDE
> ENTER ARCADE page 95

ARCADE

Dream Warriors is an arcade full of young toughs in gang colors. Their attention is currently occupied by an assortment of video games.

EXAMINE GAMES: You see a row of coin-op video games. Some of the gang members are waiting to play; they've placed quarters on the machines to reserve their place in line.

EXAMINE GANG MEMBERS: You recognize Cutter and his gang, the Southside Blades. A friendlier face is Trina "Rabbit" Rodriguez, from Los Dragóns.

EXAMINE CUTTER: He's wearing a studded leather vest, and he sports a purple mohawk. You see the handle of a switchblade in his back pocket.

EXAMINE RABBIT: She's wearing red high-top sneakers, a lightning bolt earring and a denim jacket with a dragon back patch. She's currently engrossed in getting the top score on a machine.

TALK TO SOUTHSIDE BLADES/LOS DRAGÓNS: It would be best to keep a low profile.

TALK TO CUTTER: Cutter sneers, "Get lost, pig." His gang snickers.

TALK TO RABBIT: Her eyes never leave the screen. "Hola, Slade. Wanna talk? Put up a quarter."

PUT QUARTER ON MACHINE: Rabbit starts a two-player game. She leans in close while you play. "Boss D has your partner holed up at the Harbor View docks, loading bay #23. You didn't hear it from me." She wipes the floor with you, entering "TKO" next to her high score. "Better luck next time, Slade."

ARCADE exits are:

> OUT page 94 NORTH END

MENU

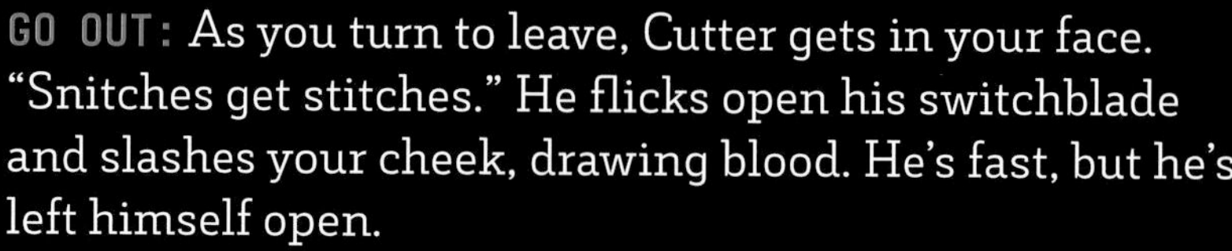

ARCADE (CONTINUED)

GO OUT: As you turn to leave, Cutter gets in your face. "Snitches get stitches." He flicks open his switchblade and slashes your cheek, drawing blood. He's fast, but he's left himself open.

HIT CUTTER WITH BAT: You hear his collarbone snap and he goes down, dropping his switchblade.

TAKE SWITCHBLADE: You pick up the knife.

Rabbit grabs your arm and whispers, "Get out of here, dummy. This isn't your fight. Go find Gheorghe. He'll fix you up."

> The player character will need to get stitched up before exploring the city on his bike. Luckily, Gheorghe is working late at his gym in Little Italy (page 97) and can offer assistance. It's a short ride—the player character can drive there despite being injured.

LITTLE ITALY

You're in a charming neighborhood where the Old World meets the new.

PARK BIKE: Most places are closed at this hour except for the coffee shop, Pixel City Café, which is open 24-7. Across the street is the boxing gym where you like to blow off steam.

ENTER CAFÉ: A bell rings as you enter the cozy coffee shop.

> The player character enters the Pixel City Café (page 99).

ENTER GYM: Gheorghe is sweeping up inside, getting ready to close up for the night. Maybe come back in the morning.

> If the player is bleeding from the fight at the arcade:

ENTER CAFÉ: Marge will kill you if you bleed all over her floor. Get patched up first, then grab a cup of joe and a side of dough.

ENTER GYM: You slump against the door and rap hard on the glass. An older man armed with a mop looks up, startled. He runs over and unlocks the door for you. He asks, "Ah, Jack, my friend... What happened?"

> The player character is brought inside Gheorghe's Gym (page 98).

LITTLE ITALY exits are:

⊠ ENTER CAFÉ page 99

⊠ ENTER GYM page 98

> DRIVE/RIDE TO GASLIGHT DISTRICT page 92

> DRIVE/RIDE TO DOWNTOWN page 100

> DRIVE/RIDE TO HARBOR VIEW page 105

> DRIVE/RIDE TO MORENA BEACH page 109

GHEORGHE'S GYM

You are inside the boxing gym. Gheorghe is here.

EXAMINE GHEORGHE: This guy coached the Romanian boxing team at the '84 Olympics. Now he owns this dump and runs a youth program to get kids off the streets and into the ring.

ASK GHEORGHE FOR HELP: He gets out a first aid kit, cleans the wound with antiseptic spray and stitches it closed. He tells you, "This will leave scar, but the way you look, it will be improvement, no?"

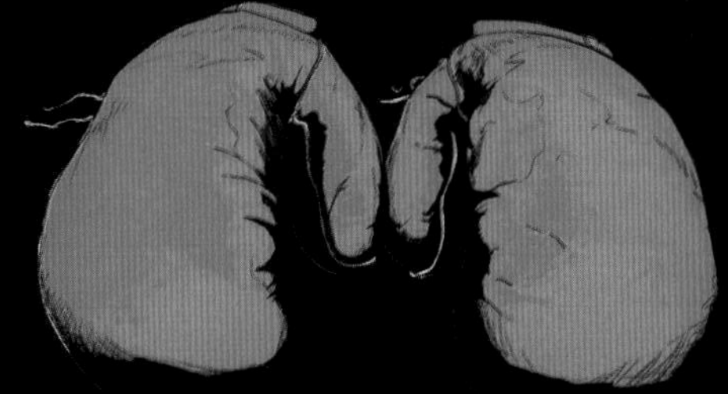

GHEORGHE'S GYM exits are:

> OUT page 97 LITTLE ITALY

PIXEL CITY CAFÉ

You're in a 24-hour coffee shop with a lunch counter and a well-lit pastry case. Marge is here. "What'll it be, hon? The usual?" she asks.

ORDER THE USUAL: You sit down at the counter, and Marge pours you a fresh cup of hot coffee. It's a lot better than yours.

DRINK COFFEE: You feel better—almost like you could single-handedly take on the Mob, rescue your partner and clean up organized crime in Santa Morena.

EXAMINE CASE: "There are some day-old donuts in the case. Was going to throw 'em out, but they're yours if you want 'em." She gives you a box of donuts.

> The player character can't eat more than one or two.

TALK TO MARGE: "I haven't seen your partner in a while. Hope she's well."

ASK MARGE ABOUT PARTNER: "You and Officer Chang are heroes around these parts! Free coffee for life. My way of saying thanks for all the good you do."

PIXEL CITY CAFÉ exits are:
> OUT page 97 LITTLE ITALY

DOWNTOWN

Downtown is home to a few struggling tech startups and Santa Morena's police department.

PARK BIKE: You're outside the police station. You see some graffiti here.

EXAMINE GRAFFITI: Someone spray painted DANGERTOWN over the slogan, "THE PIXEL CITY WELCOMES YOU!"

ENTER POLICE STATION: You pull open the door and enter.

> The player character enters the Police Station (page 101).

> After Jack Slade is shot (page 106) and the player character switches to Jetta Chang:

An ambulance is waiting for you when you arrive. The paramedics load Slade inside and rush him to the hospital.

ENTER POLICE STATION: Amid a flurry of activity, you pull open the door and enter.

> The player character enters the Police Station (page 101).

DOWNTOWN exits are:

> ENTER POLICE STATION page 101
> DRIVE/RIDE TO LITTLE ITALY page 97
> DRIVE/RIDE TO HARBOR VIEW page 105

POLICE STATION

Sergeant O'Brien is at his desk going over a stack of paperwork. You see the police chief's office and the hallway leading to the evidence locker.

> If the player character is Jack Slade:

The precinct is quiet—for once.

ENTER EVIDENCE LOCKER: You'll need someone to unlock it for you.

EXAMINE O'BRIEN: O'Brien is a middle-aged man with a bit of a paunch. He used to be the stuff of legend in Dangertown. Now he's just waiting for retirement.

TALK TO O'BRIEN: "Evening, Jack. What are you doing here? I thought the chief suspended you. I was just reading the report. You and Chang sure messed up this time."

ASK O'BRIEN ABOUT REPORT: "I'm surprised you didn't get fired. Wiretapping the mayor? Sounds like career suicide to me. You don't know when to shut up, do ya?"

ASK ABOUT CHANG: "She got off easy, if you ask me. Though it's funny... She never came in this morning for traffic duty. I tried calling. Nobody's home."

ASK O'BRIEN ABOUT TAPE: He pats his key ring. "Locked up safe and sound," he tells you.

POLICE STATION exits are:
> OUT page 100 DOWNTOWN
⊠ ENTER EVIDENCE LOCKER page 103
> ENTER CHIEF'S OFFICE page 104

POLICE STATION (CONTINUED)

ASK O'BRIEN FOR TAPE/KEYS TO EVIDENCE LOCKER: "No can do, detective. Submit a request if you need access."

SUBMIT REQUEST: He puts his feet up on his desk. "I'll get right on that."

GIVE O'BRIEN DONUTS: He says, "Slade, you're all right. I'll go grab us some coffee. Sit tight." He stands and exits the room, leaving behind his keys and the case file.

EXAMINE CASE FILE: The case file number is #198X.

EXAMINE KEY RING: You find the evidence locker's padlock key, among others.

> Taking the key ring allows a player to enter the Evidence Locker. Otherwise, it's inaccessible.

> If the player character is Jetta Chang:

O'Brien yells, "Chang! The chief wants to see you in his office right away. We're assembling a SWAT team to hit Boss D. Good work!"

EVIDENCE LOCKER

You unlock the chain-link gate and slip inside a storage area crammed with cardboard boxes, each one assigned a case number.

> The player has time to find box #198X, take the audiotape and return the keys to the sergeant's desk.

FIND BOX #198X: You find a cardboard box containing some documents, surveillance photos and a spool of reel-to-reel audiotape.

TAKE BOX #198X: Carrying the entire box out would be too conspicuous.

EXAMINE PHOTOS: Some incriminating black-and-white surveillance photos of Boss D with the mayor.

You hear footsteps approaching from down the hall...

> That's the final warning for the player to return the keys. If the player doesn't leave the Evidence Locker and return the keys to the desk:

The sergeant busts you for tampering with evidence. After a brief meeting with Internal Affairs, it's decided that you and the police department should part company. Your suspension becomes permanent. Your missing partner is never found. THE END.

EVIDENCE LOCKER exits are:

> OUT page 101 POLICE STATION

CHIEF'S OFFICE

MENU

The police chief is here at his desk.

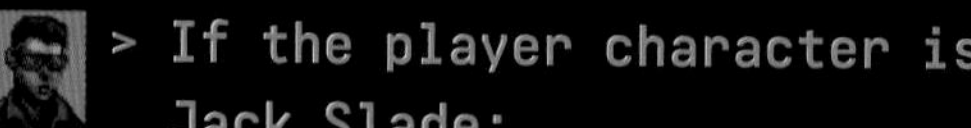
> If the player character is Jack Slade:

TALK TO CHIEF: "Dammit, Slade! I thought I gave you a two-week suspension?! Now get the hell out of my office before I make it a month!"

EXAMINE CHIEF: The chief looks exactly how you picture him, but 25 percent meaner.

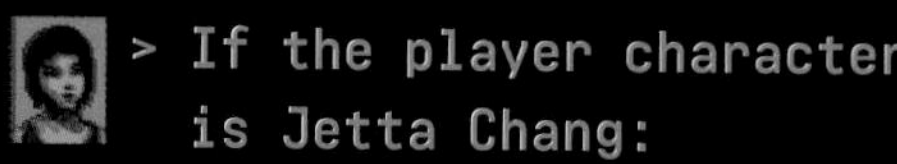
> If the player character is Jetta Chang:

There's a badge and a gun on his desk. He tells you, "Detective Chang, consider yourself back on the case. Now you get the hell out of here and do what you gotta do!"

EXAMINE BADGE: It's a Santa Morena police detective's badge. Your badge.

EXAMINE GUN: It's a loaded Beretta 92S. Your gun.

CHIEF'S OFFICE exits are:

> OUT page 101 POLICE STATION

HARBOR VIEW

You're in a rundown industrial area on the water's edge.

> If the player character is Jack Slade:

PARK BIKE: You're outside a cluster of warehouses. Some flashy sports cars are parked here.

EXAMINE WAREHOUSES: Each of the many loading bays is numbered. It would take hours to search them all.

EXAMINE CARS: You see a Porsche 911 Turbo and a Ferrari 328 GTS.

FIND BAY #23: Yeah, you see it. Just a few doors down from the cars.

ENTER BAY #23: You roll the door up and step inside.

> The player enters the Warehouse (page 106).

> If the player character uses the command SLASH TIRES, they won't be able to escape after Jack Slade is shot on page 106, and the player will lose the game!

HARBOR VIEW exits are:

> ENTER BAY #23 page 106
> DRIVE/RIDE TO MORENA BEACH page 109
> DRIVE/RIDE TO LITTLE ITALY page 97
> DRIVE/RIDE TO DOWNTOWN page 100

MENU

WAREHOUSE

The inside of the warehouse is a maze of crates and shipping containers. It's dark here, save for a single floodlight illuminating a lone woman tied to a chair.

EXAMINE WOMAN: It's your partner, Jetta Chang! She's zip-tied to a chair.

The player needs the switchblade to free Jetta.

FREE JETTA CHANG: You cut through her restraints.

Rocco emerges from the shadows, flanked by goons armed with semiautomatic pistols and submachine guns. "Slade. Give us the tape and we let you walk out of here."

EXAMINE ROCCO: Looks like you broke his nose back at the apartment.

EXAMINE GOONS: The big blond one carries a Walther PPK pistol. The smaller guy sports a Fu Manchu mustache and has an H&K MP5 submachine gun hanging from a shoulder sling.

> If the player refuses:

Rocco pulls out a Colt .45 and shoots Jetta, then you. THE END.

GIVE TAPE: You hand over the tape.

Rocco turns his back and starts to walk away, then stops. "I lied. Kill 'em both," he says. His goons march both of you behind a shipping container. The floor is covered by a plastic tarp.

> Whether the player runs, fights or tries to negotiate, the big goon shoots Slade in the stomach.

WAREHOUSE exits are:

⊡ OUT page 105 HARBOR VIEW

WAREHOUSE (CONTINUED)

> The player character is now rookie detective Jetta Chang! Read the following description:

You watch with horror as Jack catches a bullet in the gut and drops to the floor. Your limbs are sore from your long confinement, and your wrists hurt from the zip ties, but you brace for a fight that you'll probably lose. You ask yourself, Jetta, what have you gotten yourself into?

Before you can react, a young girl wearing a mask jumps down from the shipping container. She slams one of the goons with a mean right hook, then drops him with an uppercut. From behind, another goon raises his SMG to waste her.

EXAMINE GIRL: She's rocking red high-tops, hand wraps and a black domino mask.

> The girl is the vigilante known as Knockout, a.k.a. Trina “Rabbit” Rodriquez—Slade's gang contact.

ATTACK GOON: You spin-kick the goon with the Fu Manchu mustache. He goes down like a sack of bricks.

> Failing to take out the goon results in a bad end for Chang and Knockout:

You and the masked girl are riddled with bullets.
THE END.

SEARCH GOON: You find a half-eaten candy bar and keys to a Porsche.

TALK TO GIRL: “I figured dummy here would go full Rambo, so I tailed him. Get him the hell out of here and call 911 before he dies!”

DRAG SLADE OUT: You drag Slade out from Bay #23 and into the parking lot. There you find his precious Kawasaki and a white Porsche 911.

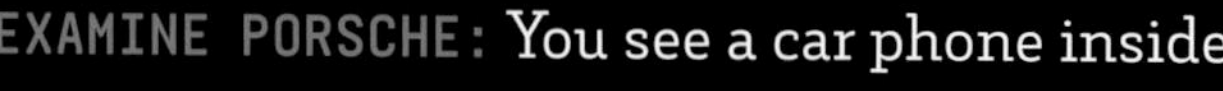

WAREHOUSE (CONTINUED)

EXAMINE PORSCHE: You see a car phone inside.

ENTER PORSCHE: It's locked.

USE KEY ON PORSCHE: You unlock the car and manage to get Slade into the passenger seat. There's a car phone here.

CALL 911 or CALL POLICE STATION: The dispatcher puts you through to the desk sergeant. "Get back downtown as soon as you can. We'll have an ambulance ready and waiting."

> The player must drive Downtown (page 100) in the Porsche before Slade bleeds out.

MORENA BEACH

You drive north up Morena Boulevard until the city lights fade from view.

> If the player character is Jack Slade:

This is where the money lives: gated communities, seaside mansions and luxury high-rises with million-dollar views. Stuff you'll never have.

PARK BIKE: From up here you can see the ocean and a whole lot of expensive real estate. Where to next?

FIND PACIFIC TOWERS: It's not hard, Pacific Towers being one of Santa Morena's tallest buildings.

ENTER PACIFIC TOWERS: Armed security guards stop you as you enter, saying, "Private property." You're strong-armed back outside to the curb.

> If the player character is Jetta Chang:

ENTER PACIFIC TOWERS: Armed security guards stop you as you enter, saying, "Private property."

SHOW BADGE: The guards let you pass. The man stationed at the front desk picks up a phone and makes a call.

MORENA BEACH exits are:

⊠ ENTER PACIFIC TOWERS page 110

> DRIVE/RIDE TO LITTLE ITALY page 97

> DRIVE/RIDE TO HARBOR VIEW page 105

PACIFIC TOWERS

MENU

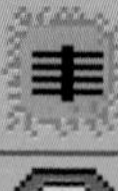
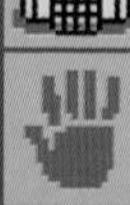

This imposing tower of concrete, glass and steel is home to Santa Morena's rich and powerful. Guards are posted in the lobby. There's an elevator here.

ENTER ELEVATOR: The doors open, and you see a very surprised Rocco Falcone. He mutters a colorful expression and reaches inside his jacket.

SHOOT ROCCO: You fire. Rocco gasps and clutches his chest, then falls. The doors close behind you.

PUNCH/KICK ROCCO: You make short work of the gangster. He'll live. The doors close behind you.

> Once Rocco is dealt with, the player has time to look around the Elevator (page 111).

> If Jetta doesn't take him out:

He draws his Colt .45 and shoots you. THE END.

PACIFIC TOWERS exits are:
> OUT page 109 MORENA BEACH
⊠ ENTER ELEVATOR page 111

ELEVATOR

You're in an elevator. There's a control panel here. Rocco's body is here.

EXAMINE CONTROL PANEL: The buttons start at L and go up to 26. At the top of the panel is a thumbprint scanner next to a button marked P.

SCAN ROCCO'S THUMB: You place Rocco's thumb on the scanner. The button lights up.

PUSH P: The elevator starts to ascend. Eventually you reach the penthouse.

SEARCH ROCCO: You find a Colt .45 pistol.

ELEVATOR exits are:
> OUT page 110 PACIFIC TOWERS
⊠ ENTER PENTHOUSE page 112

PENTHOUSE

You enter a spacious apartment all done up in chrome and white. Boss D is here, enjoying a glass of wine with the mayor of Santa Morena.

EXAMINE BOSS D: A big man wearing sunglasses, too much cologne and gold chains.

TALK TO BOSS D: "Ah, Officer Chang. Such an unexpected surprise! I heard about what happened to your partner. I do hope he pulls through."

EXAMINE MAYOR: He's nervously clutching a leather attaché case.

TALK TO MAYOR: "Uhh... Just discussing some totally legal campaign contributions!"

OPEN ATTACHÉ: There's close to a million dollars inside.

> If the player attempts to leave with the attaché case:

Is this how you thought you'd end up, just another cop on the take? This is why the bad guys always win. THE END.

SEARCH BOSS D: You find a pearl-handled Smith & Wesson .38 Special revolver and the stolen audiotape, which links him to your kidnapping. It's more than enough evidence to put him away.

> A player must search and disarm Boss D before making an arrest. If not:

Boss D draws a Smith & Wesson .38 Special, shoots you dead and escapes. THE END.

SEARCH MAYOR: You don't find anything incriminating.

SHOOT MAYOR: Although you feel the burning fires of revenge, they're not for this loser.

ARREST MAYOR: You'll need more evidence before you can arrest the mayor.

PENTHOUSE (CONTINUED)

SHOOT BOSS D: You fire your gun at point-blank range, killing Boss D in cold blood.

> Then, the game ends with this epilogue:

The SWAT team enters to find you standing over Boss D's lifeless body. The case never goes to trial, and the mayor never goes to jail. Internal Affairs launches a formal investigation but can't find anything. Still, your career is finished. You're busted down to beat cop and spend your days writing parking tickets. Slade? You see him around, but you don't talk. Yeah, you got vengeance, but did you get justice? THE END.

ARREST BOSS D: You knock Boss D down to his knees and read him his rights.

> Then, the game ends with this epilogue:

The mayor excuses himself and turns to leave when the elevator doors open and a SWAT team barges in, guns drawn and barking orders: "This is the SMPD! EVERYONE GET DOWN ON THE GROUND!"

Once the dust settles, matters go rather quickly. Boss D ends up turning witness for the prosecution, pleading down to a 20-year sentence and sending the mayor to jail.

Slade recovers from his injuries and receives the Purple Heart and an award for exceptional performance. You? You're given the Meritorious Service Award and a promotion to lieutenant.

Best of all, you get to see Jack wearing his dress uniform at the medal ceremony. You never let him live it down. THE END.

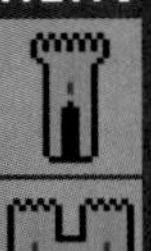

INVENTORY CHECKLIST

These items may be carried by the player:

- ☐ Leather jacket
- ☐ Slade's keys
- ☐ Newspaper
- ☐ Baseball bat
- ☐ Matchbook
- ☐ Wallet
- ☐ $100 bill
- ☐ Driver's license
- ☐ Quarter
- ☐ Switchblade
- ☐ Box of donuts
- ☐ O'Brien's key ring
- ☐ Audiotape reel
- ☐ Detective Chang's badge
- ☐ Beretta 92S
- ☐ Walther PPK
- ☐ H&K MP5
- ☐ Candy bar
- ☐ Porsche keys
- ☐ Colt .45
- ☐ Attaché case
- ☐ S&W .38 Special

SCORING: JACK SLADE

The player can earn a maximum of 65/100 points.

Playing the message on the answering machine.....+5

Reading the newspaper.................................+5

Refusing Rocco's bribe ....+5

Knocking out Rocco with the kettle..................+5

Tipping the dancers at the Tiger'z Den..............+5

Finding out Boss D's location from Cat Marco.......+5

Getting the warehouse number from Rabbit.........+5

Beating up Cutter ....+5

Getting patched up by Gheorghe ....+5

Drinking some coffee at Pixel City Café.............+5

Giving O'Brien the box of donuts.....................+5

Retrieving the audiotape from the evidence locker...+5

Freeing Jetta Chang ....+5

SCORING: JETTA CHANG

The player can earn an additional 35 points.

Helping Knockout defeat the warehouse goons ......+5

Saving Slade by getting him to the ambulance ......+5

Getting your badge and gun from the Chief ....+5

Defeating Rocco Falcone................................+5

Entering the Penthouse suite of Pacific Towers......+5

Killing Boss D. ....+0

Arresting Boss D..+5

Finishing without saving ....+5

FLAMING GOAT!
1ST
A subway commuter's routine is interrupted by a weird event. Just another day in the big city!
CONTENT RATED BY MMTRB
SURREAL
BEGINNER
EVERYONE (10+)

SUBWAY PLATFORM

You exit the train and find yourself standing all alone on a subway platform. A vending machine is here. There is an UP escalator here.

EXAMINE VENDING MACHINE: The battered and abused machine appears to be without power.

SHAKE/PUNCH/KICK VENDING MACHINE: A can of soda drops out of the machine.

EXAMINE CAN: A warm, unopened can of soda. It's dusted with an acceptable amount of rat and insect droppings.

OPEN CAN: You pop the top of the can. It lets out a pleasant "hssssss..."

DRINK SODA: You're not thirsty. Also, it's warm.

GO UP: You step onto the bottom step and are surprised to find that you go nowhere.

EXAMINE ESCALATOR: The escalator is broken. Now it is just stairs.

> The player must WALK UP the Broken Escalator.

BROKEN ESCALATOR

You are standing midway up a broken escalator. A flaming goat blocks your path.

UP/DOWN: The escalator continues to not work.

WALK DOWN: You return to the subway platform.

WALK UP: A flaming goat stands in the way.

EXAMINE GOAT: The goat is on fire. It looks angry and hungry.

POUR SODA ON GOAT: The flames are extinguished. The soda can is now empty.

> The goat is no longer angry, but it remains hungry.

FEED/GIVE CAN TO GOAT: The goat bites the can and wanders off with it, chewing noisily.

> The player character is free to WALK UP to the Top of the Broken Escalator (page 118).

TOP OF BROKEN ESCALATOR

You are standing at the top of a broken escalator. You may now resume your daily commute. What was up with that goat, eh? THE END.

SCORING

If the player character makes it to the top of the escalator, they win 1,000 points. Hurray!

JUNGLE ADVENTURE
After surviving a crash landing in the jungle, a daring archaeologist sets out to retrieve a legendary treasure.
CONTENT RATED BY MMTRB
PULP ADVENTURE
ADVANCED
EVERYONE (10+)

JUNGLE ADVENTURE MAP

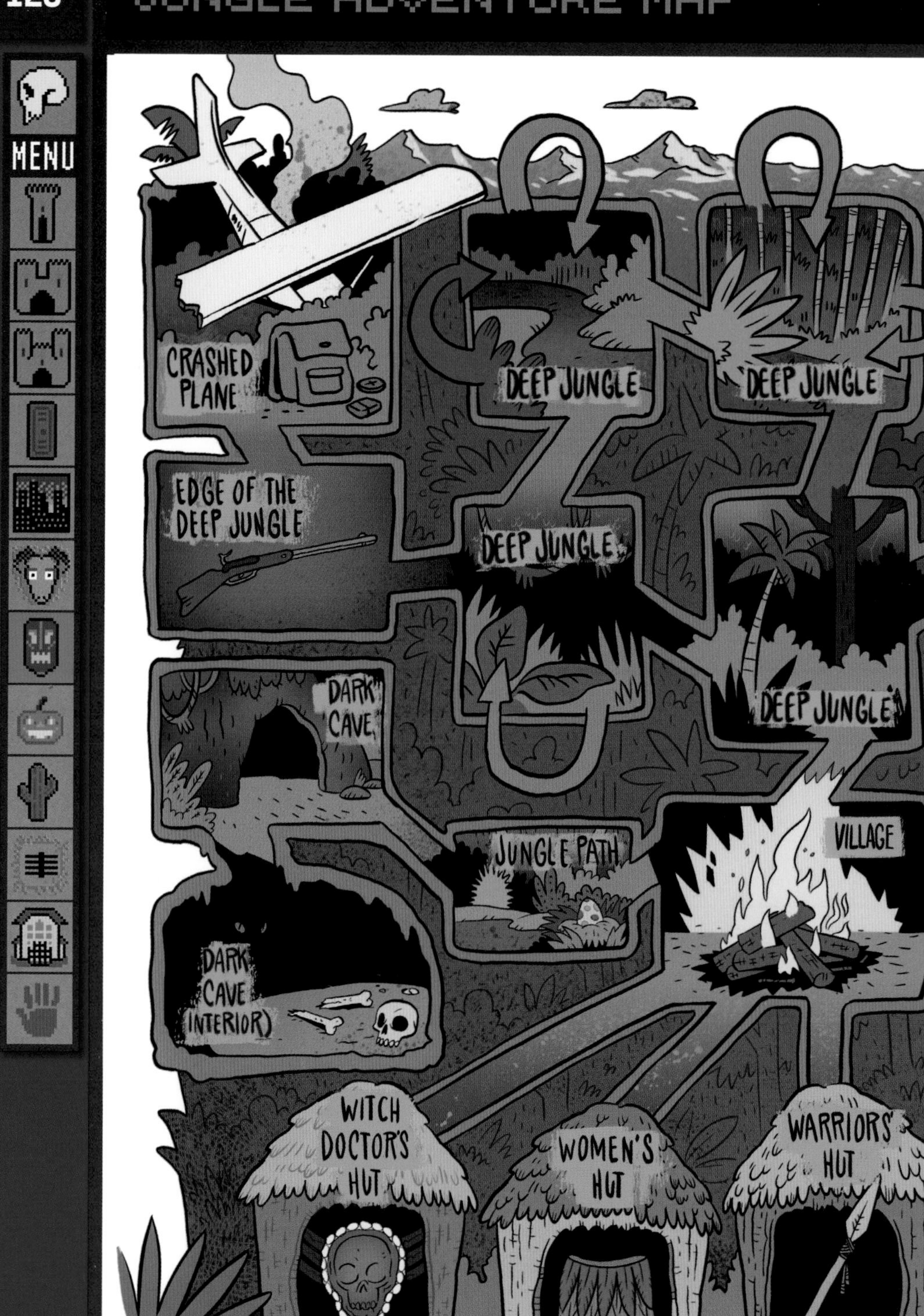

ROCKY PLATEAU
GORGE
TEMPLE OF THE GOLDEN SKULL
COOL POOL
SACRIFICIAL CHAMBER
TREASURE CHAMBER

CRASHED PLANE

MENU

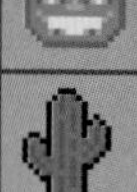

You wake up to find yourself buckled into the pilot's chair of a single-engine prop plane. Through the cockpit window you can see the deep jungle. There is a backpack here.

> The player starts the game with nothing in their inventory.

GO OUT: You're still buckled into your seat.

> Once unbuckled, the player may leave the plane.

EXAMINE BACKPACK: It contains a lighter and a compass.

> The player may WEAR BACKPACK to automatically stow any small items they find. The rifle, spear, old bones and gold skull won't fit in the pack and must be carried. The player can carry the backpack and one of these large objects or wear the backpack and carry two of these large objects.

EXAMINE LIGHTER: The silver lighter is engraved with the words, "From your colleagues at the university." You give it a shake. It's still full of lighter fluid.

> If lit, the lighter casts a flickering flame, then blows out. It's used to light a signal fire on the Rocky Plateau.

EXAMINE COMPASS: The brass compass points toward the north.

> The compass is used to navigate the Deep Jungle.

CRASHED PLANE exits are:

⊠ OUT page 123 EDGE OF THE DEEP JUNGLE

EDGE OF THE DEEP JUNGLE

You stand in a clearing, the site of a terrible plane crash. The crash site is surrounded by smoking wreckage and inhospitable jungle.

EXAMINE WRECKAGE: The plane is beyond repair, but you may be able to salvage some supplies from the wreckage.

SEARCH WRECKAGE/SALVAGE WRECKAGE: You find a rifle.

EXAMINE RIFLE: The rifle is in good condition, but it's not loaded. You find no ammunition in the wreckage.

> The rifle may be traded to the warriors in exchange for a spear.

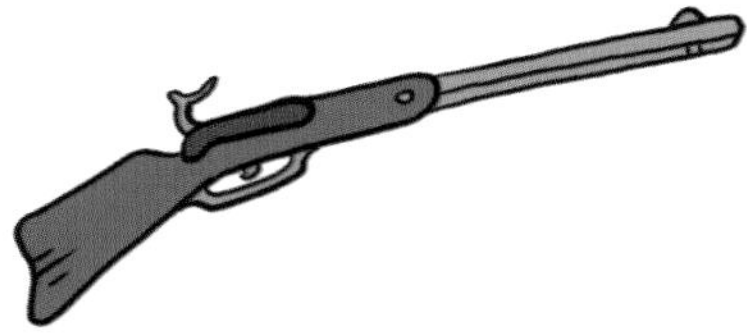

EDGE OF THE DEEP JUNGLE exits are:

> PLANE page 122 CRASHED PLANE
> JUNGLE page 124 DEEP JUNGLE

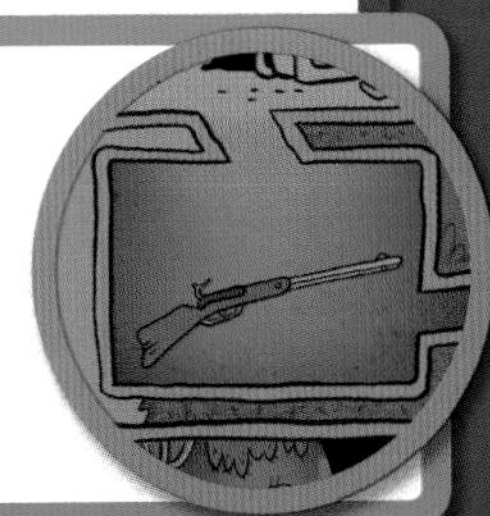

DEEP JUNGLE

MENU

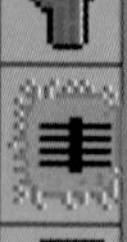

You are lost in the deep jungle.

> Each location within the Deep Jungle has four exits: NORTH, SOUTH, EAST and WEST. Some of these—marked with U-turn arrows—lead back to the previously entered area.

> If the player examines the compass while lost in the Deep Jungle, the actual exits are revealed and the U-turns are ignored.

DEEP JUNGLE EXITS ARE: 124 DEEP JUNGLE

> Using the compass, DEEP JUNGLE exits are:

NORTHWESTERN DEEP JUNGLE:

> SOUTH page 124 DEEP JUNGLE

> EAST page 124 DEEP JUNGLE

NORTHEASTERN DEEP JUNGLE:

> WEST or SOUTH page 124 DEEP JUNGLE

SOUTHEASTERN DEEP JUNGLE:

> NORTH page 124 DEEP JUNGLE

> SOUTH page 125 VILLAGE

> EAST page 131 THE GORGE

> WEST page 124 DEEP JUNGLE

SOUTHWESTERN DEEP JUNGLE:

> NORTH page 124 DEEP JUNGLE

> EAST page 124 DEEP JUNGLE

> WEST page 123 EDGE OF THE DEEP JUNGLE

VILLAGE

You enter a village. There is a cooking fire here. There are three huts here. A path leads west, and the deep jungle is to the north.

EXAMINE FIRE: The village's cooking fire burns hot and bright.

> The cooking fire is used to COOK EGG.

EAT EGG: You feel full and sleepy. You are too tired for adventure.

> The player must rest, sleep or wait before going anywhere.

EXAMINE HUTS: You see the witch doctor's hut, the women's hut and the warriors' hut.

VILLAGE exits are:

> NORTH page 124 DEEP JUNGLE

> WEST page 128 JUNGLE PATH

> ENTER WITCH DOCTOR'S HUT page 127

> ENTER WARRIORS' HUT page 126

> ENTER WOMEN'S HUT page 126

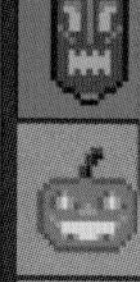

WARRIORS' HUT

You enter the warriors' hut. The warriors scowl at you and mutter to themselves, brandishing their weapons.

EXAMINE WARRIORS: These are fierce warriors armed with spears.

> Attacking the warriors is a bad idea.

> The warriors will not talk to the player. They will accept the hunting rifle as a gift and, in return, give the player a ceremonial spear.

EXAMINE SPEAR: The ceremonial spear is decorated with bird feathers and tiger teeth.

WARRIORS' HUT exits are:

> OUT page 125 VILLAGE

WOMEN'S HUT

You enter the women's hut. The women of the village greet you warmly and present you with a beaded skirt.

EXAMINE SKIRT: The beaded skirt is quite beautiful—handmade by the village women.

> The player can wear the skirt or stow it away in their pack.

WOMEN'S HUT exits are:

> OUT page 125 VILLAGE

WITCH DOCTOR'S HUT

You enter the witch doctor's hut. The village witch doctor is here.

EXAMINE WITCH DOCTOR: Which doctor? Haha. You see an ancient man. He wears a necklace made from bones and feathers. The witch doctor glares at you.

GIVE WITCH DOCTOR TIGER FANG: The witch doctor takes the fang and gives you the necklace from around his neck.

EXAMINE NECKLACE: The necklace features a bird skull surrounded by feathers. It radiates magic!

WEAR NECKLACE: You feel as light and as free as a bird! Your feet don't even leave tracks in the dirt.

SHOW/GIVE BONES: The witch doctor nods and draws a map in the dirt. He refuses the old bones.

EXAMINE MAP: A crude drawing that depicts a gorge, a temple, a skull and a strange beast.

ATTACK WITCH DOCTOR: The witch doctor curses you and flees the hut, disappearing into the jungle.

> The curse causes the player to feel the sting of a fire ant whenever any command is given.

> If the cursed player exits the Village:

As you leave the village, you are overwhelmed by a swarm of fire ants that pours out from the jungle! Your flesh is consumed by the voracious insects, and all that's left are your bones. THE END.

WITCH DOCTOR'S HUT exits are:

> OUT page 125 VILLAGE

JUNGLE PATH

You are on a jungle path that heads east-west. There is a bird's nest here.

TAKE NEST: That's someone's home!

SEARCH NEST: You find a large egg.

EXAMINE EGG: The egg is covered with green and purple spots.

> The egg may be cooked and eaten in the Village, fed to the mischievous monkey or brought back by the player for the university's ornithology department.

JUNGLE PATH exits are:
> EAST page 125 VILLAGE
> WEST page 129 OUTSIDE THE DARK CAVE

OUTSIDE THE DARK CAVE

You stand outside a dark cave. You hear the growls of a large animal from within.

ENTER CAVE: As you step into the cave, a huge tiger leaps from the shadows and pounces on you...

> If the player is unarmed:

With a savage sweep of its claws, the tiger quickly disembowels you. Then, it drags you inside to eat you. THE END.

> If the player has the spear:

Acting on pure instinct, you plunge the spear into the tiger's belly, and it falls dead.

> The player is now Inside the Dark Cave (page 130).

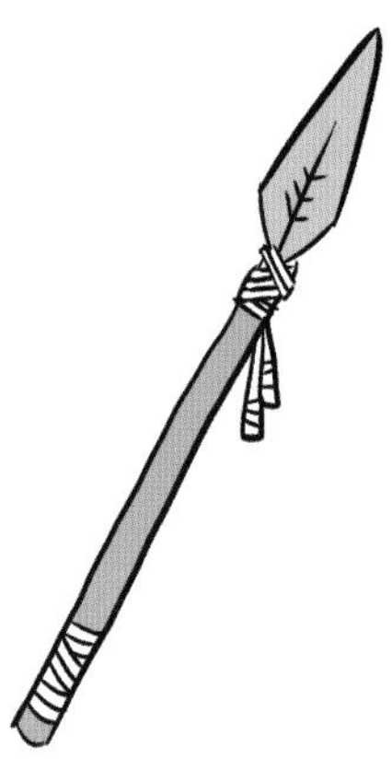

OUTSIDE THE DARK CAVE exits are:
> EAST page 128 JUNGLE PATH
⊡ CAVE page 130 INSIDE THE DARK CAVE

INSIDE THE DARK CAVE

MENU

You are inside a dark cave. It smells of tiger and death. There is a fresh tiger carcass here next to some old bones.

EXAMINE OLD BONES: The bones look to be the remains of a villager killed by the tiger.

EXAMINE TIGER: The enormous tiger is dead, impaled on your mighty spear. A broken tiger fang lies on the ground beside the tiger's body.

> The player may trade the tiger fang with the witch doctor for the necklace.

GET SPEAR: The spear is stuck in the tiger's carcass.

INSIDE THE DARK CAVE exits are:

> OUT page 129 OUTSIDE THE DARK CAVE

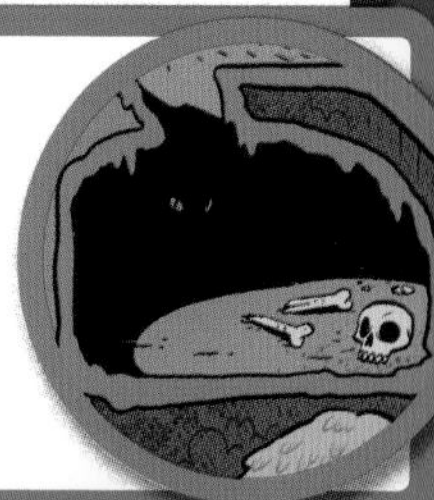

THE GORGE

You stand on the western edge of a vast, deep gorge. There's an old rope bridge here. A trail leads south.

EXAMINE GORGE: It's gorgeous! Far below, you see a winding river infested with crocodiles.

EXAMINE BRIDGE: The bridge looks quite old and creaks in the wind. I wouldn't trust it!

GO EAST or CROSS BRIDGE: The rope bridge buckles under your weight and tears free from its supports. You plunge 100 feet into the river and end up as crocodile food. THE END.

> Wearing the necklace allows the player to safely cross the bridge.

GO EAST or CROSS BRIDGE: You float over the rotting planks of the ramshackle bridge and make it to the other side, safe and sound.

THE GORGE exits are:

> SOUTH page 132 COOL POOL
⊠ EAST page 133 TEMPLE OF THE GOLD SKULL
> WEST page 124 DEEP JUNGLE

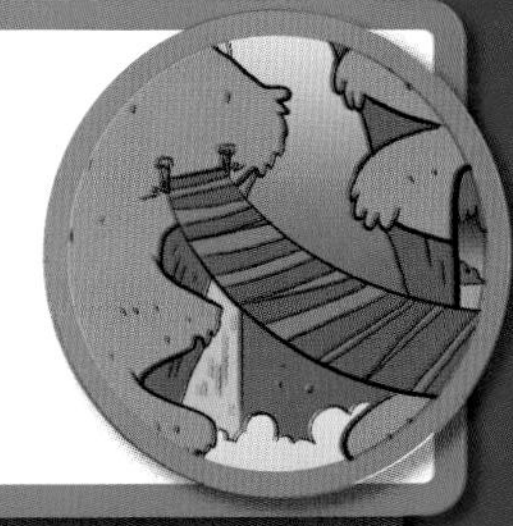

MENU

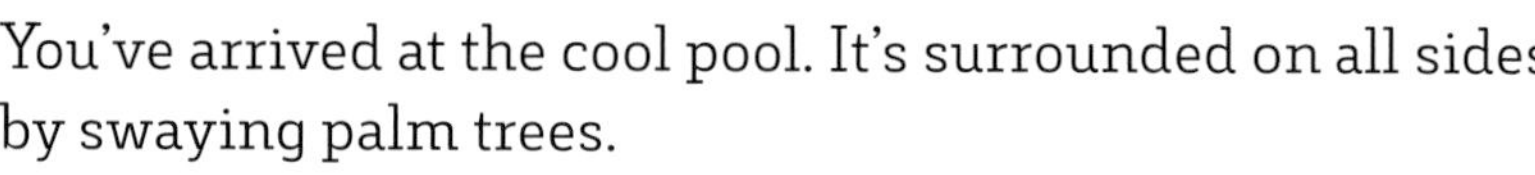

COOL POOL

You've arrived at the cool pool. It's surrounded on all sides by swaying palm trees.

> If the monkey follows the player here, it will shriek in fright and flee into the trees, dropping whatever it's carrying. It will not come down.

EXAMINE POOL: You see deadly water snakes lurking beneath the pool's tranquil waters.

ENTER POOL: As you wade into the refreshing pool, you feel something slither against your leg. Before you can react, a water snake bites into your ankle. You feel dizzy and sick, and as the poison spreads, you slip into unconsciousness. THE END.

> If the player is wearing the necklace, they may climb the palm trees, but the monkey will always scamper out of reach.

COOL POOL exits are:
> NORTH page 131 THE GORGE

TEMPLE OF THE GOLD SKULL

You stand outside the ruins of a magnificent temple. This is the mythical Temple of the Gold Skull! There is a mischievous monkey here. There's a rope bridge to the west and a clearing to the north.

EXAMINE MONKEY: The monkey could use a bath and some food. Other than that, it's quite endearing!

> The monkey is curious and cute, and will follow the player around from room to room. Each time the player enters a new room:

The noisy monkey follows you. Ook ook, eek eek!

> It will scurry out of the player's reach if an attempt is made to grab it. The monkey is easily spooked and will not enter the helicopter willingly.

> The monkey will eat a cooked egg if offered one. It will then become slow and lethargic and may be grabbed and stowed in the player's pack.

> The monkey is afraid of snakes and will hide in the trees at the Cool Pool. The monkey is light and agile enough to cross the Gorge without breaking the rope bridge.

TEMPLE OF THE GOLD SKULL exits are:
> NORTH page 134 ROCKY PLATEAU
> SOUTH page 135 SACRIFICIAL CHAMBER
> WEST page 131 THE GORGE

ROCKY PLATEAU

MENU

You stand on a wide, flat plateau. There is a thorny bush here. Far off in the distance, you can make out the sound of a helicopter. The temple lies to the south.

EXAMINE BUSH: The thorny bush is bone dry and looks like it will catch a spark quite easily.

USE LIGHTER ON BUSH: Dense smoke billows up into the sky...

> A helicopter will land after a few turns. The player may either wait for it to land or continue exploring to the south.

EXAMINE HELICOPTER: You see your old friend Jim at the controls. He waves!

> If the player wants to keep exploring, Jim will wait. After all, he's paid by the hour.

> If Jim has landed, he'll fly the player to safety once the player enters the helicopter:

Jim takes off, lifting high above the jungle canopy, and heads for home. Your Jungle Adventure is over... for now! THE END.

ROCKY PLATEAU exits are:

> SOUTH page 133 TEMPLE OF THE GOLD SKULL

SACRIFICIAL CHAMBER

You are inside the Temple of the Gold Skull. There is a stone altar here.

EXAMINE ALTAR: The altar is made of solid stone and inscribed with ancient symbols. A smooth, shallow depression is carved into the surface.

EXAMINE SYMBOLS: They point to this chamber being used for sacrificial rituals.

PUT BONES ON ALTAR: The altar slides to one side, revealing a secret tunnel that leads south.

> The player can now go south to the Treasure Chamber (page 136).

SACRIFICIAL CHAMBER exits are:

> NORTH page 133 TEMPLE OF THE GOLD SKULL

⊠ SOUTH page 136 TREASURE CHAMBER

TREASURE CHAMBER

You are in a treasure chamber. The walls are inscribed with ancient symbols. A huge statue holds a gold skull in its palm. A tunnel leads north.

> If the monkey is here:

The monkey grabs the shiny gold skull!

> The monkey will drop the skull only if it's given the egg or if it's taken to the Cool Pool.

EXAMINE SYMBOLS: An ancient warning: "Trespassers, beware!"

EXAMINE SKULL: It's made of solid gold. It belongs in a museum!

> If the skull leaves this room, the guardian statue comes to life.

EXAMINE STATUE: The stone statue is large and humanoid in appearance, combining the features of a tiger, a monkey and a human.

TREASURE CHAMBER exits are:
> NORTH page 135 SACRIFICIAL CHAMBER

TREASURE CHAMBER (CONTINUED)

> When the statue comes to life, it will chase the player from location to location, blocking all exits except those to the north.

> The player must escape the Temple of the Gold Skull and head north to the Rocky Plateau. "Get to the chopper!" If the player never lit a signal fire, the chopper won't be there to rescue the player. When the guardian reaches the Rocky Plateau:

The guardian makes sure you don't live to tell anyone tales of your jungle adventure. THE END.

> The player may temporarily escape the guardian by crossing the rope bridge—the heavy statue will not follow. But when the player crosses back over, the statue will be waiting and will chase the player north to the Rocky Plateau.

INVENTORY CHECKLIST

These items may be carried by the player:

- ☐ Backpack
- ☐ Lighter
- ☐ Compass
- ☐ Rifle
- ☐ Beaded skirt
- ☐ Egg
- ☐ Old bones
- ☐ Tiger fang
- ☐ Ceremonial spear
- ☐ Necklace
- ☐ Monkey
- ☐ Gold skull

SCORING

The player can earn a maximum of 100 points.

Note: It's possible to finish the game without finding the lost temple or the gold skull. Players must choose between the egg or the monkey, and a perfect score is only achievable by players who make it through the entire game without getting lost or killed!

Locating the Temple of the Gold Skull . . . . +10

Bringing back the gold skull for a museum's collection . . . . +30

Returning with a beaded skirt for the university's arts and culture exhibit . . . . +10

Acquiring an egg for the ornithology department . . . +5

Capturing a live monkey for the zoo . . . . +10

Navigating the deep jungle with no false exits. . . . . . . +5

Escaping the jungle in the helicopter . . . . +30

Finishing without saving . . . . +5

TOWN
THE GHOST TRAIN TO FUNLAND
YUM-YUM CANDY FACTORY
MUCKY-MUCK SWAMP
TENTACLE HIL
FOREST OF DEATH
It's Halloween, the only time that human children can visit the weird world of Pumpkin Town. Can you make it back home with a bag full of goodies?
CONTENT RATED BY MMTRB
FANTASY
BEGINNER
ALL AGES

PUMPKIN TOWN MAP

THE UNHAUNTED HOUSE

BIG TOP

TENTACLE HILL

CAULDRON POINT

FUNLAND

GHOST TRAIN

PUMPKIN TOWN

TIN SHACK

MUCKY-MUCK SWAMP

YUM-YUM CANDY FACTORY

CANDY LAB

YOUR HOUSE
ELM STREET
TRICK or TREAT
BELL TOWER
ABANDONED CATHEDRAL
GRAVEYARD
FOREST OF DEATH
PITCHFORK FARMS
GINGERBREAD FIELDS
OPEN GRAVE
SUGAR MINES
CREEPY CATACOMBS
PUMPKIN TOWN HELL

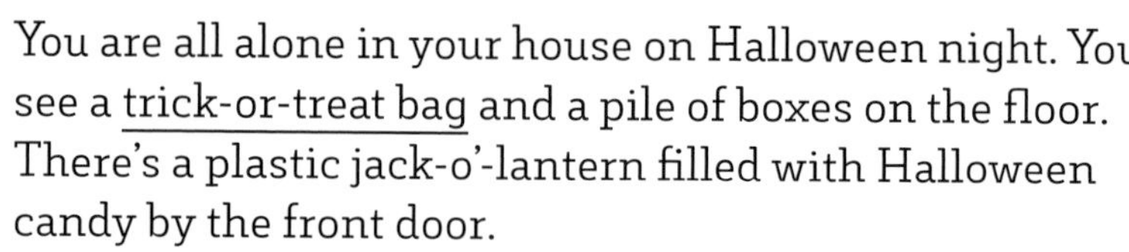

MENU

You are all alone in your house on Halloween night. You see a trick-or-treat bag and a pile of boxes on the floor. There's a plastic jack-o'-lantern filled with Halloween candy by the front door.

> The player needs to GET TRICK-OR-TREAT BAG to collect treats and score points. The SAVE GAME command will not work in this Parsely game!

EXAMINE JACK-O'-LANTERN: Inside the plastic pumpkin are individually wrapped pieces of bubble gum.

TAKE BUBBLE GUM: You grab a handful of bubble gum.

EXAMINE BOXES: The boxes contain Halloween costumes your mom brought down from the attic. One is a vintage witch costume, one is an official "Pirate Bill" costume and the last one is labeled "Action Spooky Ghost Costume" in felt-tipped marker.

> The player may take only one costume.

EXAMINE WITCH COSTUME: It contains a long black gown, a pointy black hat and an old-timey broom.

> The vintage witch can FLY TO anywhere in Pumpkin Town if the location is known.

EXAMINE PIRATE COSTUME: It's got a cool eye patch, an awesome pirate hat and a wicked hook hand.

> Pirate Bill can use his hook hand to fight the giant squid and to retrieve the coin.

EXAMINE GHOST COSTUME: It's just a white sheet with eyeholes. Lame!

> The ghost costume makes the player invisible.

YOUR HOUSE exits are:
> OUT page 143 ELM STREET

ELM STREET

You are outside your house on Elm Street. It is late, and all the houses are dark except for your neighbor's house across the street. There is a storm drain here.

EXAMINE STORM DRAIN: Looking down through the grate, you half expect to see a razor-fanged clown emerge from the shadows. Instead, you spy the glint of a coin!

GET COIN: Your hand is too big to fit through the narrow grate.

CHEW GUM: You chew the bubble gum until it loses its flavor and your jaw hurts.

STICK GUM ON HOOK: You stick the wad of gum on the end of your hook hand.

USE HOOK ON COIN: You reach through the narrow grate with your hook and stick the gum to the coin. You now have a coin!

EXAMINE COIN: A silver coin—heads is a jester's cap, tails is the word "FUNLAND."

ENTER NEIGHBOR'S HOUSE: Maybe you should knock first?

KNOCK ON DOOR: You are greeted by an elderly couple holding a bowl of candy.

ELM STREET exits are:
> HOME page 142 YOUR HOUSE
⊡ BONE LADDER page 145 MAIN STREET, PUMPKIN TOWN

ELM STREET (CONTINUED)

EXAMINE COUPLE: It's your neighbors, the Parsons.

EXAMINE BOWL: It's almost empty. You see some pieces of candy corn.

> If the player is wearing a costume:

"Oh, aren't you a cute little {witch/pirate/ghost}!"

SAY TRICK OR TREAT: They give you the last of their candy: some stale candy corn. Your neighbors say good night, shut the door and turn off their lights.

> If the player is not wearing a costume:

Your neighbors yell at you for "horsing around," then close and lock their door and turn off the light.

They will not answer the door again!

> Once the lights are off:

A mysterious ladder drops from the night sky!

EXAMINE LADDER: You see a ladder made of... bones? It rises high into the sky.

CLIMB LADDER: Do you really want to leave Elm Street?

SAY NO: You ignore the spooky ladder for now.

SAY YES: You climb. Halfway up, you look down and see that Elm Street is gone. Where are you? Maybe it's time to go back...?

GO DOWN/CLIMB DOWN: You're standing on an unfamiliar street. Welcome to Pumpkin Town!

MAIN STREET, PUMPKIN TOWN

You are in the center of Pumpkin Town. Exits lead in every direction. Fortunately, there's a signpost here. There is a bone ladder here, hanging in midair.

EXAMINE SIGNPOST: It points to several destinations...

NORTH: Cauldron Point

NORTHWEST: Tentacle Hill

SOUTH: Yum-Yum Candy Factory

SOUTHEAST: Pitchfork Farms

SOUTHWEST: Mucky-Muck Swamp

EAST: The Forest of Death

WEST: Ghost Train to Funland

> The player can GO in any of these directions.

EXAMINE LADDER: The bone ladder rises high into the sky.

CLIMB LADDER: Do you really want to leave Pumpkin Town?

SAY NO: You ignore the spooky ladder for now.

SAY YES: You climb. Halfway up, you look down and see that Pumpkin Town is gone. You become dizzy, your fingers slip from the ladder and you seem to fall for an eternity. You wake up in bed, clutching your trick-or-treat bag! Was it all a dream? THE END.

MAIN STREET, PUMPKIN TOWN exits are:

⚄ BONE LADDER page 142 YOUR HOUSE

> NORTH page 149 CAULDRON POINT

> NORTHWEST page 148 TENTACLE HILL

> SOUTH page 146 YUM-YUM CANDY FACTORY

> SOUTHEAST page 159 PITCHFORK FARMS

> SOUTHWEST page 150 MUCKY-MUCK SWAMP

> EAST page 156 FOREST OF DEATH

> WEST page 152 GHOST TRAIN

YUM-YUM CANDY FACTORY

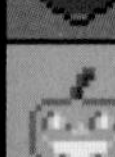

You feel like a kid in... in some kind of a store. There doesn't seem to be anyone working today except for a prickly security guard sitting outside the candy lab.

EXAMINE GUARD: The guard's green skin is covered in cactus spines. He's reading a newspaper.

ENTER CANDY LAB: "Sorry, the factory is closed for Halloween."

SHOW ID TO GUARD: The guard glances blankly at your ID, not even looking up. "Working late, Norm? Go on in."

If the player character is wearing the ghost costume, they can sneak into the Candy Lab (page 147) unseen.

YUM-YUM CANDY FACTORY exits are:

> OUT page 145 MAIN STREET

⊠ ENTER CANDY LAB page 147

CANDY LAB

The lab is filled with all sorts of weird equipment: hydrometers, thermometers, beakers, Bunsen burners and tumblers. You see a jawbreaker and a whiteboard.

EXAMINE WHITEBOARD: You see a message that reads, "Norm, our prototype for the 'Yum-Yum Candy Exploding Jawbreaker' is ready for testing. Do not drop it!"

EXAMINE JAWBREAKER: You see a baseball-sized jawbreaker covered in sparkles and swirls.

> A player who drops the jawbreaker or tries to eat it will explode and wake up in the Graveyard (page 155).

CANDY LAB exits are:

> OUT page 146 YUM-YUM CANDY FACTORY

TENTACLE HILL

MENU

You can see all of Pumpkin Town from the top of this hill. There is a normal-looking house here. A car is parked in the driveway.

EXAMINE HOUSE: The house is oddly normal, with a picket fence, well-trimmed lawn and a welcome mat outside the front door. It's an un-haunted house!

EXAMINE CAR: You see a modern-looking car, the only one you've seen in town so far. Through the window you spy an ID badge hanging from the rearview mirror.

EXAMINE ID BADGE: The ID reads, "Norman Johnson, Yum-Yum Marketing."

ENTER HOUSE: The door is locked. Perhaps you should ring the doorbell?

RING BELL: You ring the bell and hear a voice say, "Just a moment!" When the door opens, a pretty woman dressed in an apron greets you. She is holding a tray of warm chocolate chip cookies. "Oh my, look at you! How scary!"

SAY TRICK OR TREAT: She gives you some homemade chocolate chip cookies, then says goodbye and closes the door.

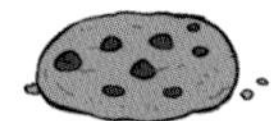

TENTACLE HILL exits are:
> SOUTHEAST page 145 MAIN STREET

CAULDRON POINT

You walk along until you come to a beach by a bubbling lake. A fishy-looking lifeguard is here, sitting in a high wooden chair. Bats fly overhead in lazy circles.

EXAMINE LAKE: It's actually a huge, bubbling kettle that's half-buried in the ground. From time to time, a tentacle erupts from beneath the surface and plucks a bat out of the sky.

EXAMINE LIFEGUARD: The scaly fellow is wearing a whistle around his neck and some swim trunks. "S'up, bro? I'm Gill."

THROW JAWBREAKER AT TENTACLE: The tentacle is not there—whatever's in that lake is submerged below the surface.

ENTER LAKE: A tentacle grabs you from below and pulls you down beneath the surface of the water!

 If the player is wearing the pirate costume or carrying the pitchfork:

You jab at the tentacle and it lets go. Gill is impressed by your bravery and offers you a bag of gummi worms.

> Otherwise:

You struggle but are no match for the tenacious tentacle. All of a sudden, you feel someone pulling you to safety—it's Gill! He loads you into a hearse, and you're taken to the graveyard to recuperate.

> Go to the Graveyard (page 155). Gill closes the beach and won't let anyone enter for safety reasons. If the player tries to reenter Cauldron Point, a sign reads, "BEACH CLOSED UNTIL FURTHER NOTICE."

CAULDRON POINT exits are:
> SOUTH page 145 MAIN STREET

MUCKY-MUCK SWAMP

MENU

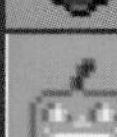

You arrive at the edge of a dark, sinister swamp. Pools of molasses bubble up from the ground and tangled black licorice whips hang from the chocolate trees. Glowing red eyes watch you from the shadows.

GET LICORICE: Do you really like black licorice, or are you just trying to score more points?

> If the player insists, give them some. They can use the licorice whip on the devil.

GET CHOCOLATE: You scavenge some dark chocolate bark and bittersweet twigs from the trees.

> The player can use the bucket to acquire a bucket of molasses. It doesn't count as a treat, but it can be used to trap a gingerbread person in Gingerbread Fields (page 160).

ENTER SWAMP: Do you dare enter the swamp?

SAY NO: Smart! You're safe... for now.

> If the player says YES and has the candy cane:

Feeling your way through the treacherous swamp with the candy cane, you come across a tin shack.

> Go to the Tin Shack (page 151).

> If the player says YES and doesn't have the candy cane:

You foolishly wander around the swamp and fall into a sticky pool of molasses. It sucks you under and you pass out. When you awaken, you're in the graveyard. Your ruined costume is gone, and you're now dressed as a hobo.

> Go to the Graveyard (page 155).

MUCKY-MUCK SWAMP exits are:
> NORTHEAST page 145 MAIN STREET
⊡ SWAMP page 151 TIN SHACK

TIN SHACK

You're in a derelict shack. Inside is a table and a bottle of butterscotch.

EXAMINE BOTTLE: The bottle is half-full. Or half-empty, depending on your outlook.

DRINK BOTTLE: You take a swig of the butterscotch. Oooooh, that's the good stuff!

TIN SHACK exits are:
> OUT page 150 MUCKY-MUCK SWAMP

GHOST TRAIN

MENU

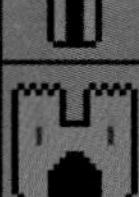

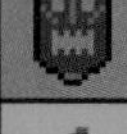

You're on the ghost train platform at Pumpkin Town Station. There's a sign here. You see a vial lying on the ground.

EXAMINE VIAL: The vial contains sparkly purple, red and gold pixie dust. It must be, like, 99 percent pure sugar. How vile...!

EAT PIXIE DUST: You instantly go into sugar shock and collapse. A hearse is called for, and it soon arrives, sirens blaring. You're taken to the graveyard for detox.

> Go to The Graveyard (page 155).

EXAMINE SIGN: The sign reads "This way to Funland!" with an arrow pointing west.

GO WEST: You need to board the ghost train.

BOARD TRAIN: The conductor blocks your path. "Fare, please!"

> A player without the fare will be booted from the train by the conductor. The ghost can sneak on board without paying. The witch can fly to Funland using the broom. The hobo can show the hobo nickel to ride for free.

GIVE COIN TO CONDUCTOR: You climb aboard the ghost train. After a while, you find yourself approaching the circus tents and amusement park rides of Funland!

> Go to Funland (page 153).

GHOST TRAIN exits are:

> EAST page 145 MAIN STREET
⊠ BOARD TRAIN page 153 FUNLAND
> FLY TO FUNLAND page 153 FUNLAND

FUNLAND

You're in the midway of Funland, an old carnival. In front of you is a circus tent. The snack witch is here. You see the ghost train waiting here to return you to Pumpkin Town.

EXAMINE WITCH: The snack witch is an old woman dressed in a black gown and pointy hat. She sells cotton candy and shiny red apples from her cart.

EXAMINE COTTON CANDY: It's pink and blue spun sugar on a cone.

ASK FOR/BUY COTTON CANDY: "One coin, please!"

EXAMINE APPLES: These shiny apples are definitely safe to eat.

> The apple isn't a treat, so it's not worth any points.

ASK FOR/BUY APPLE: "For you, free of charge!" The witch cackles. She gives you an apple.

> If the player is dressed as a witch, the old witch will not give out any apples. Instead, she says:

"Oh dearie... you should really know better!"

EAT APPLE: *crunch!* Oh no, those are definitely not safe to eat! You feel sick to your stomach, and the world starts to go blurry...

> The player awakens in the Graveyard (page 155).

FUNLAND exits are:
> EAST page 152 GHOST TRAIN
> TENT page 154 INSIDE THE BIG TOP

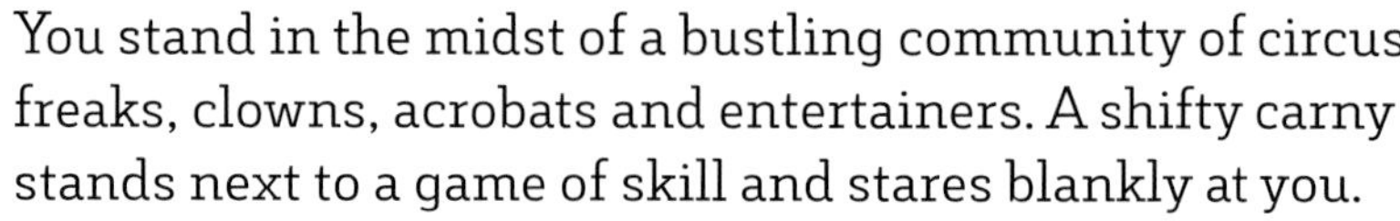

INSIDE THE BIG TOP

MENU

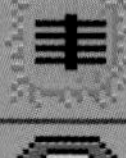

You stand in the midst of a bustling community of circus freaks, clowns, acrobats and entertainers. A shifty carny stands next to a game of skill and stares blankly at you.

EXAMINE CARNY: The carny is wearing dirty overalls and is missing some teeth. He points at a booth and says in a creepy drawl, "Play a game, win a prize."

EXAMINE BOOTH/GAME: "Knock down three bottles with a beanbag, win a prize. Easy as pie."

> The game costs a coin per beanbag. The carny will give the player a free throw for a swig of the butterscotch.

PLAY GAME: "You get one throw for one coin, pal."

GIVE CARNY COIN: He gives you a suspiciously light beanbag.

GIVE BUTTERSCOTCH TO CARNY: "Don't mind if I do!" He takes a swig and hands it back. "Here, have a free throw."

THROW BEANBAG: The beanbag bounces off the bottles. "Better luck next time," drawls the carny. He takes a swig from a flask of something and chuckles to himself.

THROW JAWBREAKER: It explodes! The heavy milk bottles are sent flying. The carny reluctantly hands over a bag of orange circus peanuts.

EXAMINE CIRCUS PEANUTS: The grossest candy in the world. Still, at least you won something!

INSIDE THE BIG TOP exits are:
> OUT page 153 FUNLAND

GRAVEYARD

You're in the graveyard, where the townsfolk go to recover from a lack of Halloween spirit. The night nurse is standing beside an open grave. There is a bucket here. There is a cane here.

> Players who fall victim to calamitous incidents will wake up here.

EXAMINE BUCKET: It looks freshly kicked.

EXAMINE CANE: It's a red-and-white-striped peppermint candy cane.

EXAMINE NURSE: She's wearing a white dress with a red skull and crossbones on the front. Her name tag reads, "Abby Cadaver."

TALK TO NURSE: "Oh, dear! You're looking positively alive! How dreadful!"

> After a squid attack or molasses drowning, the nurse gives the player a hobo costume to replace their ruined one. A character wearing the hobo costume can ride the rails for free.

EXAMINE SELF/COSTUME: You're wearing a bowler hat, bow tie and tattered, floppy shoes. Your bindle contains a hobo nickel and a can of beans.

EXAMINE GRAVE: You look down into the open grave, but you can't see the bottom!

ENTER GRAVE: You jump into the grave and slide down a twisting chute all the way to the creepy catacombs!

> The player drops down into the Creepy Catacombs (page 162).

GRAVEYARD exits are:
> WEST page 157 ABANDONED CATHEDRAL
> ENTER GRAVE page 162 CREEPY CATACOMBS

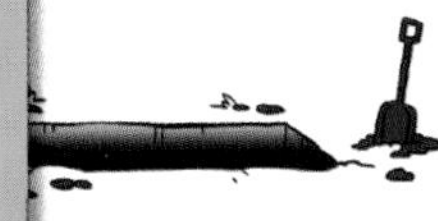

FOREST OF DEATH

Through the gloom you make out the shape of a bell tower rising from the trees. You hear owls hoot at you from the shadows, and a cold, icy fear grips your very soul. Dare you enter the forest of death?

> If the player enters the forest:

A Nameless Primal Dread fills you! If you got lost, you'd be all alone in that dark place and never make it back home! If only there were a way to mark a trail...

MARK TRAIL: What do you want to use to mark a trail?

> A player can mark a trail using the candy corn, circus peanuts or red-hot cinnamon hearts.

Now you can find your way back if you get lost!

Summoning your courage, you continue onward to the abandoned cathedral.

FORESТ OF DEATH exits are:
⊠ EAST page 157 ABANDONED CATHEDRAL
> WEST page 145 MAIN STREET

ABANDONED CATHEDRAL

You wander through the crumbling cathedral and marvel at its gothic beauty. A rickety staircase leads up to the bell tower. The trail east leads to the graveyard.

> The bell ringer appears here when he's on his snack break.

CLIMB STAIRS: You climb up the rickety staircase until you reach the top of the bell tower.

> Go to the Bell Tower (page 158).

ABANDONED CATHEDRAL exits are:

> EAST page 155 GRAVEYARD
> WEST page 156 FOREST OF DEATH
> UP page 158 BELL TOWER

BELL TOWER

MENU

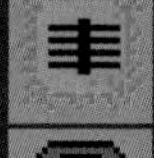

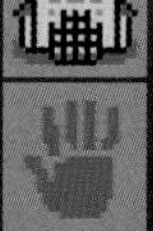

From above, you hear the rustling of leathery wings in the belfry. There's a graveyard to the east. The forest of death lies to the west. A bell ringer is here, standing beside a pull rope.

EXAMINE BELL RINGER: You have a hunch that he works here.

TALK TO BELL RINGER: "Is it snack time yet?"

RING BELL/PULL ROPE: The bell ringer stands in front of the rope. "Oi! Get your own bell!"

GIVE COOKIES: "Oooh! Cookies! But can't have cookies without milk!" He pushes them away.

GIVE MILK: "Ahhh! Milk! But can't have milk without cookies!" He pushes it away.

GIVE MILK AND COOKIES: The bell ringer heads downstairs to take his snack break.

> The bell ringer will also take the tin of beans if it's offered to him.

"Oooh, baked beans—the magical fruit!"

> After the bell ringer leaves, the player may then ring the bell.

RING BELL/PULL ROPE: The bell rings loudly, disturbing a bat living in the belfry. It flies away, dropping the gingerbread person it was carrying.

EXAMINE GINGERBREAD PERSON: Five-second rule! An arm broke off, but it otherwise looks okay.

BELL TOWER exits are:

> DOWN page 157 ABANDONED CATHEDRAL

PITCHFORK FARMS

This farm raises candy corn, candy pumpkins, marshmallow chicks and zombie cows. You hear giggling and screaming to the east.

EXAMINE CORN/PUMPKINS: The crops were already harvested for Halloween.

EXAMINE CHICKS: They hop around and make peeping noises.

TAKE CHICKS: It's no use trying to pick up chicks here! They scurry off to a peep show.

USE PITCHFORK ON CHICKS: You impale some marshmallow chicks.

EXAMINE COW: A cow moos in a sickly fashion and shambles over to be milked.

> If the player has a bucket from the Graveyard, the cow may be milked:

MILK COW: You get a bucket of milk.

PITCHFORK FARMS exits are:
> NORTHWEST page 145 MAIN STREET
> EAST page 160 GINGERBREAD FIELDS

GINGERBREAD FIELDS

MENU

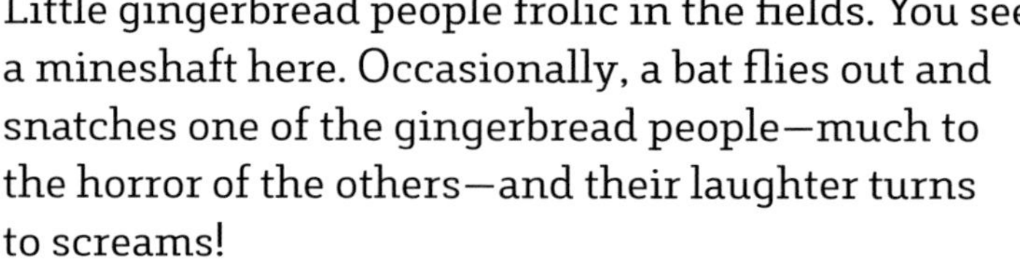

Little gingerbread people frolic in the fields. You see a mineshaft here. Occasionally, a bat flies out and snatches one of the gingerbread people—much to the horror of the others—and their laughter turns to screams!

EXAMINE GINGERBREAD PEOPLE: The gingerbread people sing, dance and play in the fields.

TAKE GINGERBREAD: The gingerbread person laughs, "Can't catch me!" and runs away. A bat swoops down, grabs it and flies off toward the abandoned cathedral.

USE/POUR MOLASSES: The sticky syrup covers the ground and snares a gingerbread person as they try to run across it!

ENTER MINESHAFT: You head down into the twisting, narrow tunnels of the sugar mines.

GINGERBREAD FIELDS exits are:
> WEST page 159 PITCHFORK FARMS
> DOWN page 161 SUGAR MINES

SUGAR MINES

Zombie miners patrol the twisting tunnels, searching for veins of rock candy. A passage up leads out of the mines, and the creepy catacombs await you to the east.

EXAMINE ZOMBIES: You see shambling corpses wearing helmets and carrying picks. Some of them appear to have suffered miner injuries.

TALK TO ZOMBIES: Hey! Mine your own business!

ATTACK ZOMBIES: Leave 'em alone. Can't you see they're miners?

EXAMINE ROCK CANDY: Do you know the street value of this stuff?

MINE ROCK CANDY WITH PICKAXE: You chip off a good-sized chunk of blue rock candy.

SUGAR MINES exits are:
> EAST page 162 CREEPY CATACOMBS
> UP page 160 GINGERBREAD FIELDS

CREEPY CATACOMBS

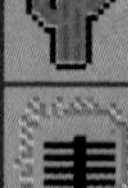

You're in the creepy catacombs, a network of tunnels beneath Pumpkin Town. It looks like one of the tunnels has collapsed—debris litters the ground. An arched passage leads farther south into the unknown.

EXAMINE DEBRIS: Beneath a pile of fallen rocks, you see a twitching hand. It holds a pickaxe.

EXAMINE PICKAXE: You could probably take it; the owner doesn't seem to need it anymore.

EXAMINE PASSAGE: The arch reads: "Abandon all hope, ye who enter here!" You see flickering lights and feel intense heat emanating from the tunnel.

CREEPY CATACOMBS exits are:
> SOUTH page 163 PUMPKIN TOWN HELL
> WEST page 161 SUGAR MINES

PUMPKIN TOWN HELL

Little devils with pitchforks dance around gouts of flame to old-time jazz music. This place is uncomfortably hot! A large devil wearing a suit and tie approaches you as you enter Pumpkin Town Hell.

EXAMINE DEVIL: He's holding a pitchfork and a crystal goblet filled with red-hot cinnamon hearts.

TALK TO DEVIL: He holds out a goblet of red-hot cinnamon hearts and asks, "Tell me, have you been a good little {witch/ghost/pirate/hobo/human} this Halloween?"

SAY NO: The devil gives you a handful of red-hot cinnamon hearts.

SAY YES: "THEN GET OUT!" He kicks you out, back to the creepy catacombs.

> If kicked out, the player may come back in a different costume and trick the devil.

WHIP DEVIL: He yelps and drops his pitchfork. "I'm a bad devil! Haha, that was fun! Do it again!"

> The player won't get anything else out of the devil.

PUMPKIN TOWN HELL exits are:

> NORTH page 162 CREEPY CATACOMBS

INVENTORY CHECKLIST

These items may be carried by the player:

- ☐ Trick-or-treat bag
- ☐ Witch costume (broom)
- ☐ Pirate costume (hook hand)
- ☐ Ghost costume
- ☐ Bubble gum
- ☐ Funland coin
- ☐ Candy corn
- ☐ Jawbreaker
- ☐ ID badge
- ☐ Chocolate chip cookies
- ☐ Gummi worms
- ☐ Black licorice whips
- ☐ Dark chocolate bark and twigs
- ☐ Butterscotch
- ☐ Pixie dust
- ☐ Cotton candy
- ☐ Poisoned apple
- ☐ Beanbag
- ☐ Circus peanuts
- ☐ Hobo costume (bindle contains tin of beans and hobo nickel)
- ☐ Empty bucket
- ☐ Bucket of molasses
- ☐ Bucket of milk
- ☐ Candy cane
- ☐ Gingerbread person
- ☐ Marshmallow chicks
- ☐ Pickaxe
- ☐ Rock candy
- ☐ Pitchfork
- ☐ Cinnamon hearts

SCORING

The player can earn a maximum of 100 points:

Returning from Pumpkin Town . . . . +5

Bonus Points for Treats:

Bubble gum. . . . . +5

Candy corn . . . . +5

Yum-Yum Candy Exploding Jawbreaker. . . . . +5

Chocolate chip cookies . . . . +5

Gummi worms . . . . +5

Black licorice whips . . . . +5

Dark chocolate bark and twigs . . . . +5

Butterscotch . . . . +5

Pixie dust. . . . . +5

Cotton candy . . . . +5

Circus peanuts . . . . +5

Peppermint candy cane. . . . . +5

Gingerbread person . . . . +5

Marshmallow chicks . . . . +5

Blue rock candy. . . . . +5

Red-hot cinnamon hearts. . . . . +5

BONUS POINTS FOR AVOIDING THESE PITFALLS

Not being kicked off the Ghost Train . . . . +5

Not being kicked out of Pumpkin Town Hell . . . . +5

Not taking an emergency trip to the Graveyard. . . . . . +5

SKULLTRONIC][

```
]LIST
10 GR
20 COLOR = 15
30 FOR N = 8 TO 20
40 HLIN 17,23 AT 7: HLIN 17,23 AT 6
50 HLIN 15,25 AT N
60 NEXT
70 FOR N = 21 TO 26
80 HLIN 17,23 AT N
90 NEXT
100 COLOR = 0
110 FOR N= 11 TO 16
120 HLIN 17,19 AT N
130 HLIN 21,23 AT N
140 NEXT
150 HLIN 20,20 AT 18: HLIN 19,21 AT 19
160 HLIN 19,21 AT 20
170 PLOT 18,24: PLOT 20,24: PLOT 22, 24
180 PLOT 18,25: PLOT 20,25: PLOT 22, 25
190 PLOT 18,26: PLOT 20,26: PLOT 22, 26
200 PRINT "HELLO, WORLD!": END

]
```

WANTED

SIX-GUN SHOWDOWN

The disgraced former sheriff of a one-horse town embarks on a mission of revenge and redemption. Bar brawls, rattlesnakes, abandoned gold mines and gunslingers await!

CONTENT RATED BY MMTRB

WESTERN

EXPERIENCED

TEEN (13+)

SIX-GUN SHOWDOWN MAP

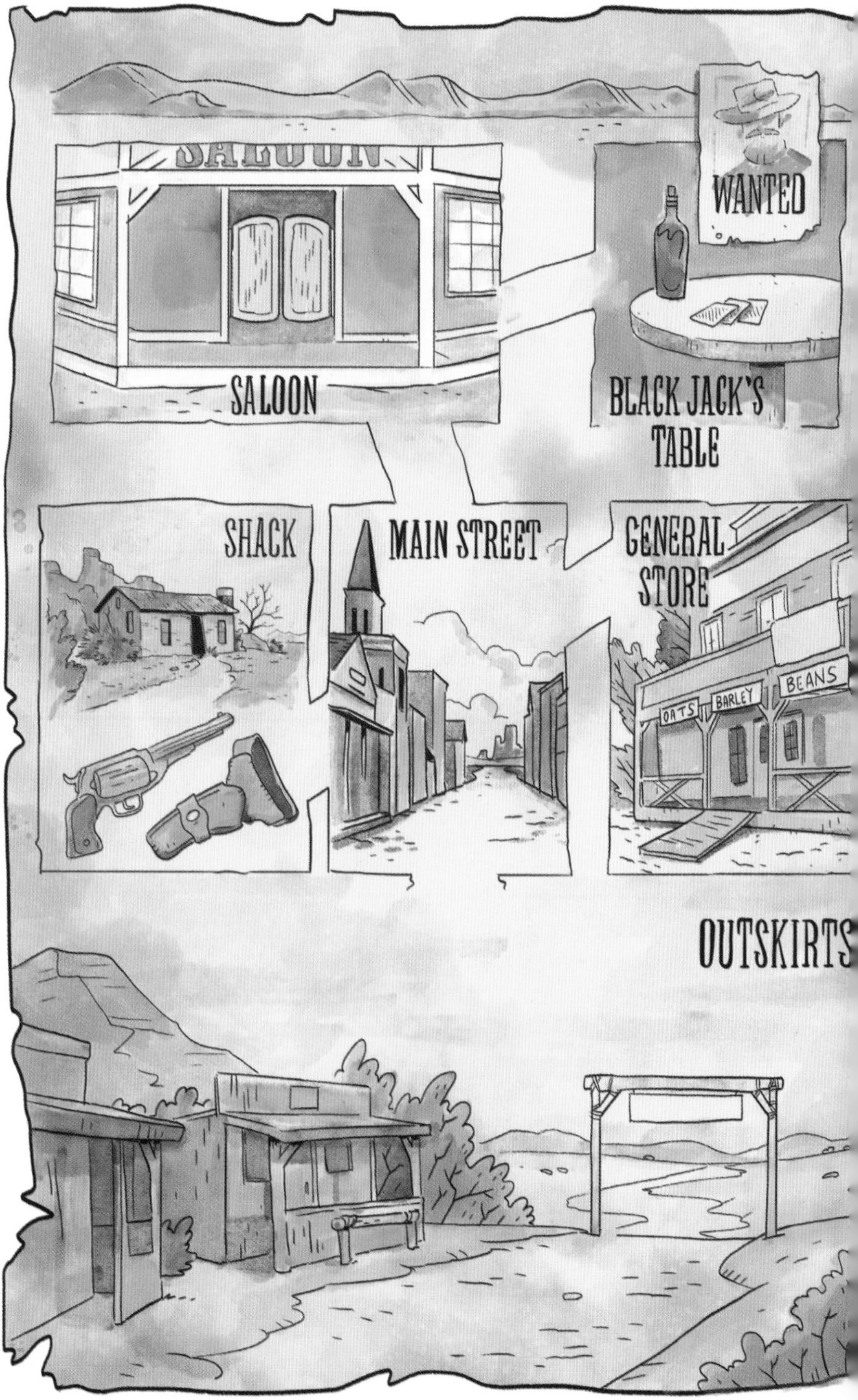

SALOON

BLACK JACK'S TABLE

SHACK

MAIN STREET

GENERAL STORE

OATS

BARLEY

BEANS

OUTSKIRTS

DESERT
DESERT
DOC HENSLEY'S
WAGON
Doc Hensley's Fabulous Elixir
DESERT
DESERT
DARK CAVE
PARSON'S CLAIM
DESERT
DESERT
CAMPSITE

MAIN STREET

MENU

You're fresh out of the drunk tank, down to a pair of worn leather boots and whatever's left in your pockets. The saloon and general store are here. Your shack is to the west. A road leads south to the edge of town.

> The player starts the game with a badge, a penny and a pair of leather boots.

EXAMINE POCKETS: You find your pa's old silver sheriff's badge and a copper penny. Your hands are shakin' like the devil—seems a little hair of the dog is required. Fortunately, you still have that bottle back at home.

EXAMINE BADGE: Your pa's badge. He was a good man who kept the peace in this town. You still remember the day a cattle rustler shot him in the back and took his life.

WEAR BADGE: The tremor in your hands makes even this simple task impossible.

EXAMINE PENNY: Quite literally your last cent. That, plus a dwindling line of credit at Cooper's General Store, is the sum of your worldly fortune.

MAIN STREET exits are:
- > NORTH page 172 SALOON
- > SOUTH page 177 OUTSKIRTS OF TOWN
- > EAST page 176 GENERAL STORE
- > WEST page 171 RUNDOWN SHACK

RUNDOWN SHACK

You stagger back home to your shack. Home sweet home. Pa's pistol and holster are here, hanging on a hook. There's a broken whiskey bottle on the floor.

EXAMINE PISTOL/HOLSTER: That's as fine a piece of steel as there ever was. You check the cylinder... and it's still loaded, for old times' sake. But your gunslinger days are far behind you.

WEAR PISTOL/HOLSTER: You sling the pistol onto your hip. The belt buckle is tricky, what with your hands shaking so much from your affliction.

EXAMINE BOTTLE: Yep, that might explain last night's sleeping arrangements.

RUNDOWN SHACK exits are:
> OUT page 170 MAIN STREET

SALOON

MENU

Drinking in public was never your style, but desperate times call for desperate measures. You belly up to the bar. The bartender gives you a polite nod and continues to polish a shot glass. "What'll it be?"

ORDER DRINK: The bartender says, "Sarsaparilla's one cent, friend." He won't sell anything harder to a drunk like you.

BUY SARSAPARILLA: You pay, and the bartender slides the bottle down to you. You now have a bottle of sarsaparilla.

EXAMINE BOTTLE: Not the kind of drink you were after...

DRINK BOTTLE: Mmm... refreshing. The bottle is now empty.

> After the player takes a drink, the bartender leans in:

"You'd best be careful. Black Jack Baker is still mighty sore from when your pa brought the law down on him and his gang." You follow his gaze over to a table toward the back of the saloon.

EXAMINE TABLE: Black Jack is sitting there with a motley crew of desperadoes. There's a wanted poster laid out across their table.

SALOON exits are:
> OUT page 170 MAIN STREET
⊠ BLACK JACK'S TABLE page 174

SALOON (CONTINUED)

EXAMINE POSTER: You can't see the details from here.

EXAMINE BLACK JACK: Black Jack is idly carving into the tabletop with his trusty bowie knife.

As his eyes meet yours, he stands up. "Well, well. How the mighty have fallen. Why don't you sit yourself down and play a hand with me and the boys, for old times' sake?" It doesn't look like he's asking.

> The player character must take a seat at Black Jack's Table and play a hand of poker (go to page 174).

BLACK JACK'S TABLE

MENU

Black Jack shuffles a ragged deck of cards. "Ante up. What's your wager?"

GO OUT: One of Black Jack's men insists that you finish the hand. He pats his sidearm.

WAGER LIFE: "Seems you did that when you sat down at the table. Now, ante up."

WAGER PISTOL: Pa's pistol? You can't part with that!

WAGER BOOTS: No offense, but nobody wants those old things.

WAGER BADGE: Black Jack nods, and he pockets your badge. He deals the cards. "If you win, we let you walk away." You now have a hand of cards.

EXAMINE CARDS: An ace, a pair of deuces and a pair of fours. Not a bad hand. Black Jack asks you, "So? Fold, draw or call?"

CHEAT: You may be a lot of things, but you ain't no cheat.

FOLD/QUIT: You fold your hand, sighing in despair. Black Jack laughs. His gang throws you out of the bar. As you lie there in the dirt, you realize that old badge was the last thing to remind you of who you once were. Without it, you're nothin'. THE END.

BLACK JACK'S TABLE exits are:
⊠ OUT page 170 MAIN STREET

BLACK JACK'S TABLE (CONTINUED)

DRAW: You discard, drawing another deuce... a full house!

> Either two pair or a full house will beat Black Jack's pair of queens.

BLUFF/CALL/CHECK: You put on your best poker face and call.

After player BLUFFS, CALLS OR CHECKS: Black Jack stares at you a good long while, then grins. "Pair o' ladies," he says and puts down two queens. When you show your hand, he flies into a rage and draws his bowie knife. "You dirty, snake-in-the-grass, chislin' cheat!"

SHOOT BLACK JACK: You fumble for your pistol—too slow! Black Jack is quicker on the draw and hurls his bowie knife into your chest, killing you dead. THE END.

HIT BLACK JACK WITH BOTTLE: You smash the bottle over his cranium, knocking him out cold. His bowie knife clatters onto the table next to the wanted poster.

A shotgun blast rings out from the bar as the bartender attempts to restore decorum. Black Jack's men scatter, one pausing to heave his boss from the table and carry him outside.

EXAMINE POSTER: You see a depiction of Black Jack Baker's scowling face. But turning the poster over reveals a crude map of the badlands.

EXAMINE MAP: A meandering line runs from town and ends at a drawing of a cave. This'll be handy if you go out into the desert.

> If the player lingers:

The bartender frowns, "I think you better pack up and go." He motions toward the door.

STAND/LEAVE: You head back outside to Main Street.

> Go to Main Street (page 170).

GENERAL STORE

MENU

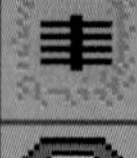

Mariah Cooper, the proprietress of this establishment, takes one look at you and frowns. "The usual? A bottle of whiskey and a can of beans?" There are various supplies and sundries here.

EXAMINE MARIAH: She's a winsome woman dressed in a shopkeeper's apron.

EXAMINE SUPPLIES: The store has everything you'd need for traveling through the badlands. You even spy the old white Stetson you traded in for a bottle of something.

BUY {ITEM}: "Wind up your tab and we'll talk."

SHOW MAP TO MARIAH: "That's the old Parson claim! They say it's long since dried up, but if you're fool enough to walk 10 miles through desert, I'll give you some supplies so you don't die out there. In return, I get a share of whatever you find. Agreed?"

SAY YES: Mariah spits in her hand and offers it to you. "Deal!"

SHAKE HAND: You seal the deal, and she gives you a rucksack.

EXAMINE RUCKSACK: It contains much-needed supplies: a flint and steel, a bedroll, a tin of beans and a full canteen.

GENERAL STORE exits are:
> OUT page 170 MAIN STREET

OUTSKIRTS OF TOWN

You head out on foot with the sun beating down on your head, wishing that you never traded your hat for a bottle of hooch. The badlands stretch out before you.

> If the player tries to enter the Desert without supplies:

Gonna venture out into the badlands without food, water or fire? Where'd you grow up, New York City?

OUTSKIRTS OF TOWN exits are:

> NORTH page 170 MAIN STREET
⚄ SOUTH page 178 DESERT

DESERT

MENU

This time of day, all the critters are sleeping underground to keep out of the sun. And here you are, wandering around the desert like a darn fool.

EXAMINE MAP: Looks like you should go west until you find a cluster of creosote bushes.

> Rules for Thirst: The player has enough water for three drinks of water while out in the Desert. Whenever the player takes a drink, mark off one drink of water.

You drink sparingly from the canteen, trying to save some for later.

> If the player is prompted to drink water but travels on without drinking:

Tired and parched, you sit down to rest. A lizard runs over your foot, looks up at you and says, “Howdy, pardner!” Surely that can’t be right.

> If the player travels on without drinking again:

You collapse and perish. THE END.

DESERT exits are:
> NORTH page 177 OUTSKIRTS OF TOWN
> WEST page 179 DESERT (CREOSOTE BUSHES)

DESERT (CREOSOTE BUSHES)

Miles out into the desert, you're heartened to see a cluster of creosote bushes as depicted on the map. You sure could use a drink right now.

DRINK: You drink sparingly from the canteen, trying to save some for later.

EXAMINE BUSHES: The dry, scraggly brush would make good tinder for building a fire.

TAKE BRUSH/TINDER: It's a simple matter to collect tinder from the dry-as-a-bone creosote bushes.

EXAMINE MAP: There's a drawing of a cactus south of the creosote bushes.

DESERT (CREOSOTE BUSHES) exits are:
> EAST page 178 DESERT
> SOUTH page 180 DESERT (LONELY CACTUS)

MENU

DESERT (LONELY CACTUS)

After another couple of hours of walking, you arrive at a lonely cactus with two arms jutting from its sides.

CUT CACTUS: You cut into the cactus and catch some precious drops of water in your canteen.

> This gives the player one extra ration of water.

EXAMINE MAP: Looks like there should be a river to the east.

DESERT (LONELY CACTUS) exits are:
> NORTH page 179 DESERT (CREOSOTE BUSHES)
> EAST page 180 DESERT (ARROYO)

DESERT (ARROYO)

You meander down the length of a bone-dry arroyo, alert for signs of flash flooding. Speaking of water, you sure could use a drink right about now.

DRINK: You drink sparingly from the canteen, trying to save some for later.

EXAMINE MAP: Keep walking south until you happen across a pine tree.

DESERT (ARROYO) exits are:
> SOUTH page 181 DESERT (PINE TREE)
> WEST page 180 DESERT (LONELY CACTUS)

DESERT (PINE TREE)

You see a gnarled bristlecone pine. This might be a good place to make camp. The sun's going down, and it gets mighty cold out here in the desert.

> The player must MAKE CAMP before continuing east.

EXAMINE TREE: The lower branches would make good firewood.

TAKE BRANCHES/FIREWOOD: It's a simple matter to break off some branches for firewood.

MAKE CAMP: You hunker down for the night.

> Go to the Campsite (page 182).

EXAMINE MAP: To the east is a sketch of a cow skull.

DESERT (PINE TREE) exits are:
> NORTH page 180 DESERT (ARROYO)
> MAKE CAMP page 182 CAMPSITE
⊠ EAST page 184 DESERT (COW SKULL)

CAMPSITE

You're hungry, cold, tired and, darn it, your feet hurt.

> The player must build a fire, cook the beans and then get some sleep.

> First, they need tinder and firewood to start a fire. The map cannot be used as tinder; it's needed to find Parson's claim.

BUILD FIRE: You build a small nest of creosote and lay down the pine branches.

> This depletes the fire-building materials.

USE FLINT AND STEEL: Your hands shake so much that it takes several tries, but you manage to get a fire started. After a while, you no longer feel cold.

COOK BEANS: Mmm, mmm. Smells like heaven.

EAT BEANS: You no longer feel hungry. Maybe it's time to get some shut-eye.

SLEEP: Aw, heck. Your feet hurt from walking all day, and you just can't get settled.

> The player must remove their boots.

TAKE OFF BOOTS: Ahhh... So much better. Your feet no longer hurt.

SLEEP: You stretch out on your bedroll and fall into an uneasy sleep.

CAMPSITE exits are:

⊠ LEAVE/BREAK CAMP page 181
DESERT (PINE TREE)

CAMPSITE (CONTINUED)

Your eyes blink open to the sight of the sun rising in the distance. Looks like you can get a head start on the day and beat the heat.

LEAVE CAMP: You best put on your boots first. That desert sand can get mighty hot.

WEAR BOOTS: You fail to notice the rattlesnake sleeping in your boot. Its fangs sink into your foot, and after a few painful hours, you die. THE END.

EXAMINE BOOTS: You see a sleeping rattlesnake coiled up inside your left boot.

SHAKE BOOT: A mean-looking rattlesnake falls out, and you drop your boot in surprise. The varmint coils up, hisses and rattles its tail.

SHOOT SNAKE: Your hands are shaking too much to get off a clean shot!

KILL SNAKE WITH KNIFE: You hack at the snake and manage to clumsily separate its head from its body. Just to be safe, you bury the head in the ground like a good cowboy. There's now a headless rattlesnake here.

TAKE SNAKE: You pack up the dead rattler. Them's good eatin'.

WEAR BOOTS: You slip on your boots. Time to break camp and mosey on outta here.

BREAK/LEAVE CAMP: You pack up your gear and kick some sand over the embers of your fire.

> The player returns to the Desert (Pine Tree) on page 181.

DESERT (COW SKULL)

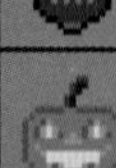

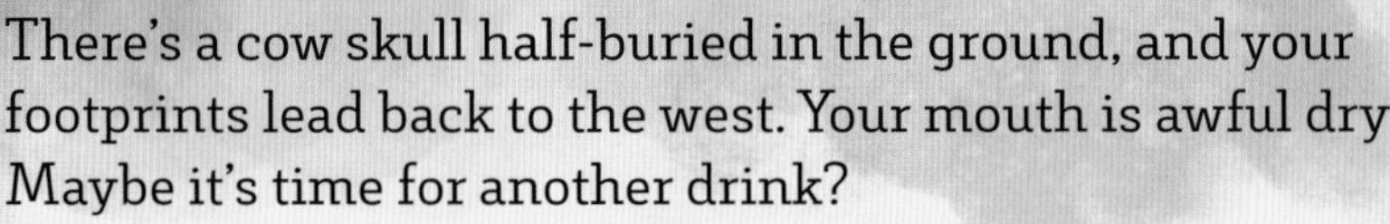

There's a cow skull half-buried in the ground, and your footprints lead back to the west. Your mouth is awful dry. Maybe it's time for another drink?

> At this point, the player is either out of water or has just a few sips left:

DRINK: You drink sparingly from the canteen, trying to save some for later.

> or

DRINK: And… now it's gone. How the heck are you gonna make it back to town?

EXAMINE MAP: Almost there! Just keep walking north until you reach a rocky bluff. That's where X marks the spot.

DESERT (COW SKULL) exits are:
> NORTH page 185 ROCKY BLUFF
> WEST page 181 DESERT (PINE TREE)

ROCKY BLUFF

You walk until you reach what looks to be the rocky bluff depicted on the map. This must be Parson's claim! There's a small cave entrance here.

EXAMINE CAVE: The crevice is small and low to the ground. It'll be a tight squeeze, but you can get inside if you drop your rucksack and crawl in on your hands and knees.

> The player character must leave their rucksack outside if they want to enter.

ROCKY BLUFF exits are:

⊠ NORTH page 188 DOC HENSLEY'S WAGON

> SOUTH page 184 DESERT (COW SKULL)

⊠ CAVE page 186 DARK CAVE

DARK CAVE

MENU

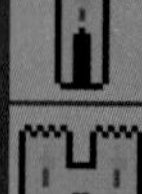

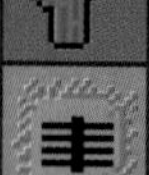

The sunlight from outside doesn't do much to illuminate the cramped cave. You can't see more than a few feet in front of you.

LIGHT FIRE: Doesn't seem to be anything here to burn, pardner.

> The player must bring in the map and flint and steel from their pack.

BURN MAP: You spark flint and steel and set the map ablaze, turning it into a makeshift torch. The light illuminates the cave.

SEARCH CAVE: The floor here is mostly sand blown in from the desert. You belly-crawl toward the back and spy a mound of dirt and sand near the far wall.

DIG: You drop the torch and burrow into the sand like a prairie dog, digging up a small leather pouch! Then your fire dies, leaving you in darkness.

EXAMINE POUCH: It's too dark to see anything!

GO OUT: You emerge from the cave, blinking in the morning sun. When your vision clears, you can just barely make out a cloud of dust to the north.

EXAMINE POUCH: It contains a small fortune in gold nuggets. You're rich!

DARK CAVE exits are:
> OUT page 185 ROCKY BLUFF

DARK CAVE (CONTINUED)

EXAMINE DUST CLOUD/LOOK NORTH: You see a buckboard wagon rolling across the desert to the north.

GO NORTH/HAIL DRIVER: You walk north and hail the driver. He pulls on the reins and halts his wagon.

The driver looks down and tips his hat. "Top o' the mornin' to you," he says from the driver's seat. "You're a bit far from home, yes?"

EXAMINE WAGON: A clapboard sign on the side of the wagon reads "Doc Hensley's Fabulous Elixir" in flowing script.

EXAMINE DRIVER: He's an elderly dude dressed in a suit, tie and bowler hat.

TALK TO DRIVER: "Fancy that! Didn't reckon I'd meet another soul in this inhospitable wilderness. Doc Hensley's the name, and the healing arts are my stock-in-trade. You look like you could use some assistance, in matters both medicinal and transportive. Climb aboard!"

CLIMB ABOARD/GO WAGON: You clamber up onto the wagon beside Doc Hensley.

> Go to Doc Hensley's Wagon (page 188).

DOC HENSLEY'S WAGON

You travel for a few hours, making small talk with the doctor. He agrees to take you back to town, seeing as it's not too far out of the way. You spy an open crate among Doc Hensley's other supplies.

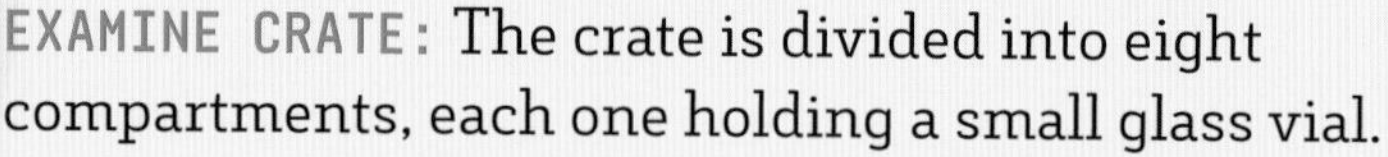

EXAMINE CRATE: The crate is divided into eight compartments, each one holding a small glass vial.

EXAMINE VIAL: It's labeled, "Doc Hensley's Fabulous Elixir," otherwise known as "snake oil."

> The snake oil is required to cure the player's shaky hands.

Doc Hensley pulls a vial from the crate and shows it to you. "My fabulous elixir is a remedy for all manner of ailments, from gout and tuberculosis to arthritis and snakebite... and only 10 cents a bottle!"

GIVE GOLD TO DOC: "Either you're attempting to swindle me with fool's gold, or you're soft in the head. Either way, I decline!"

GIVE SNAKE TO DOC: "Ah yes, a crucial component for this healing concoction. Seems like a fair trade to me!" Doc Hensley hands you a vial of the snake oil.

DRINK SNAKE OIL: "Don't drink it, friend. It's for topical use."

USE SNAKE OIL ON HANDS: You rub the elixir into your skin. The oily substance smells foul, but it makes your hands tingle with warmth. Your stiff fingers relax and your tremors fade away!

> Once the player has the elixir, regardless of whether or not it was used, go to the Main Street Clock Tower (page 189).

MAIN STREET CLOCK TOWER

Doc drops you off at the outskirts of town, and you hike back to Main Street. There, you find Black Jack Baker and his gang waiting for you under the old clock tower.

Black Jack steps forward. "Well, howdy, pardner. Seems you got the drop on me back there. Ain't gonna happen again." His men snicker; you see scatterguns and rifles poorly concealed under their dusters.

> If the player refuses to fight, Black Jack's gang takes care of business:

Black Jack's gang strips you of your possessions and leaves you bloody, beaten and shamed in the street. THE END.

TALK/CHALLENGE/DUEL BLACK JACK: "Think you're faster than me? Not a chance."

> The player must apply the snake oil to their hands to cure their tremors and have any chance at winning the upcoming duel.

A crowd gathers. Mariah watches from her shop window. Behind you, the clock's hands creep toward noon as the sun rises in the sky.

> Go to the Six-Gun Showdown (page 190).

THE SIX-GUN SHOWDOWN

MENU

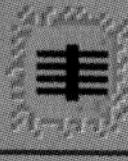

> The player and Black Jack stand on Main Street, staring each other down. It's a waiting game; whoever fires first is going to lose—you're fast, but he's faster.

SHOOT BLACK JACK: Black Jack sees you reach for your pistol and draws. You're fast, but he's faster. The bullet catches you in the stomach, and you die in the dirt like a dog. THE END.

WAIT or EXAMINE {character/object}: The sun climbs higher into the sky, peeking up over the clock tower. Black Jack squints in the harsh glare of the sun.

SHOOT/DRAW AND FIRE: With lightning speed, you draw steel and fire while the sun is in Black Jack's eyes. He grunts in surprise and keels over, dead as a doornail. His men make themselves scarce pronto, and the crowd erupts in cheers!

Mariah runs out from her shop to greet you.

GIVE GOLD/SHOW GOLD TO MARIAH: "Wasn't sure you'd be back. Even less sure you'd keep your word if you found anything out there. Seems I had you all wrong... sheriff." She reaches into Black Jack's pocket and retrieves your pa's badge.

WEAR BADGE: You pin the badge on your chest. The Law is back in town. THE END.

INVENTORY CHECKLIST

These items may be carried by the player:

- [x] Boots (worn)
- [x] Penny
- [x] Badge
- [ ] Pistol and holster
- [ ] Bottle
- [ ] Bowie knife
- [ ] Wanted poster/ treasure map
- [ ] Rucksack
- [ ] Flint and steel
- [ ] Bedroll
- [ ] Tin of beans
- [ ] Canteen of water
- [ ] Cactus water
- [ ] Tinder
- [ ] Firewood
- [ ] Dead rattlesnake
- [ ] Pouch of gold nuggets
- [ ] Snake oil

SCORING

The player can earn a maximum of 100 points:

Strapping on your pistol and holster . . . . +5
Ordering a bottle of sarsaparilla . . . . +5
Anteing your badge in the poker game. . . . . +5
Winning the poker game with two pair . . . . +5
Winning the poker game with a full house . . . . +10
Finding the treasure map . . . . +5
Procuring some supplies from Mariah Cooper. . . . . . . +5
Cutting open the cactus to get more water. . . . . +5
Checking your boot for snakes . . . . +5
Killing the rattlesnake . . . . +10
Finding the buried pouch of gold nuggets . . . . +10
Curing your ailment with the snake oil . . . . +5
Defeating Black Jack Baker and his gang . . . . +10
Squaring up your account with Mariah . . . . +5
Becoming the sheriff . . . . +10
Finishing without saving . . . . +5

SPACE STATION
You wake from cryonic suspension aboard a space station to discover you're under attack! Can you find a way to escape?
CONTENT RATED BY MMTRB
SCIENCE FICTIO
EXPERIENCED
EVERYONE (10+)

SPACE STATION MAP

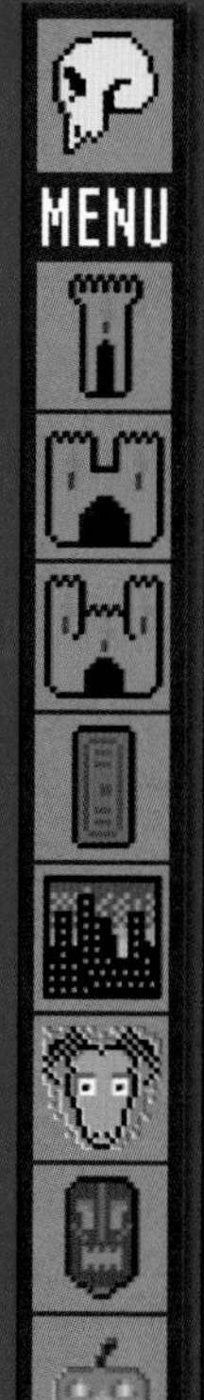

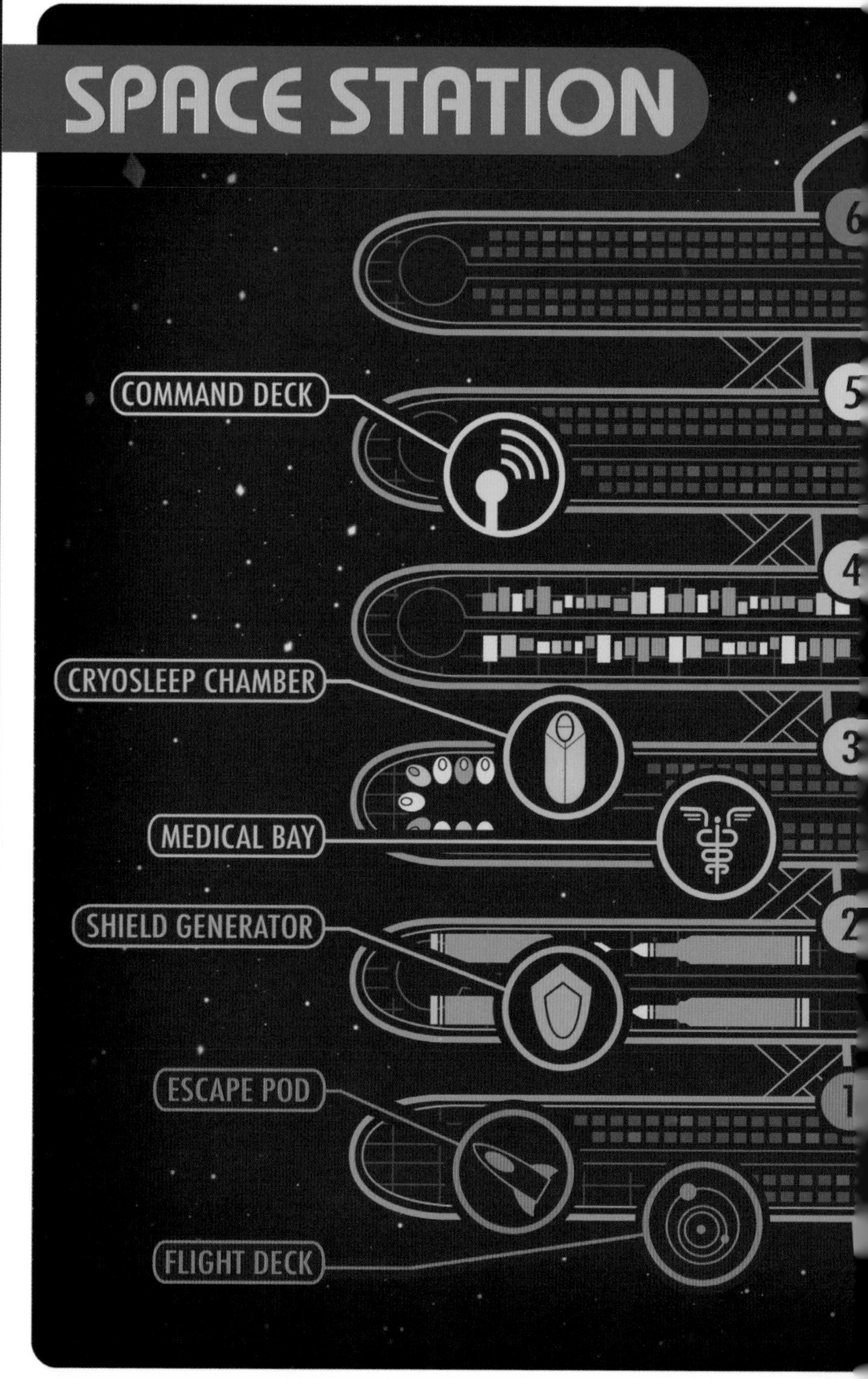

SPACE STATION

6

5

COMMAND DECK

4

CRYOSLEEP CHAMBER

3

MEDICAL BAY

2

SHIELD GENERATOR

1

ESCAPE POD

FLIGHT DECK

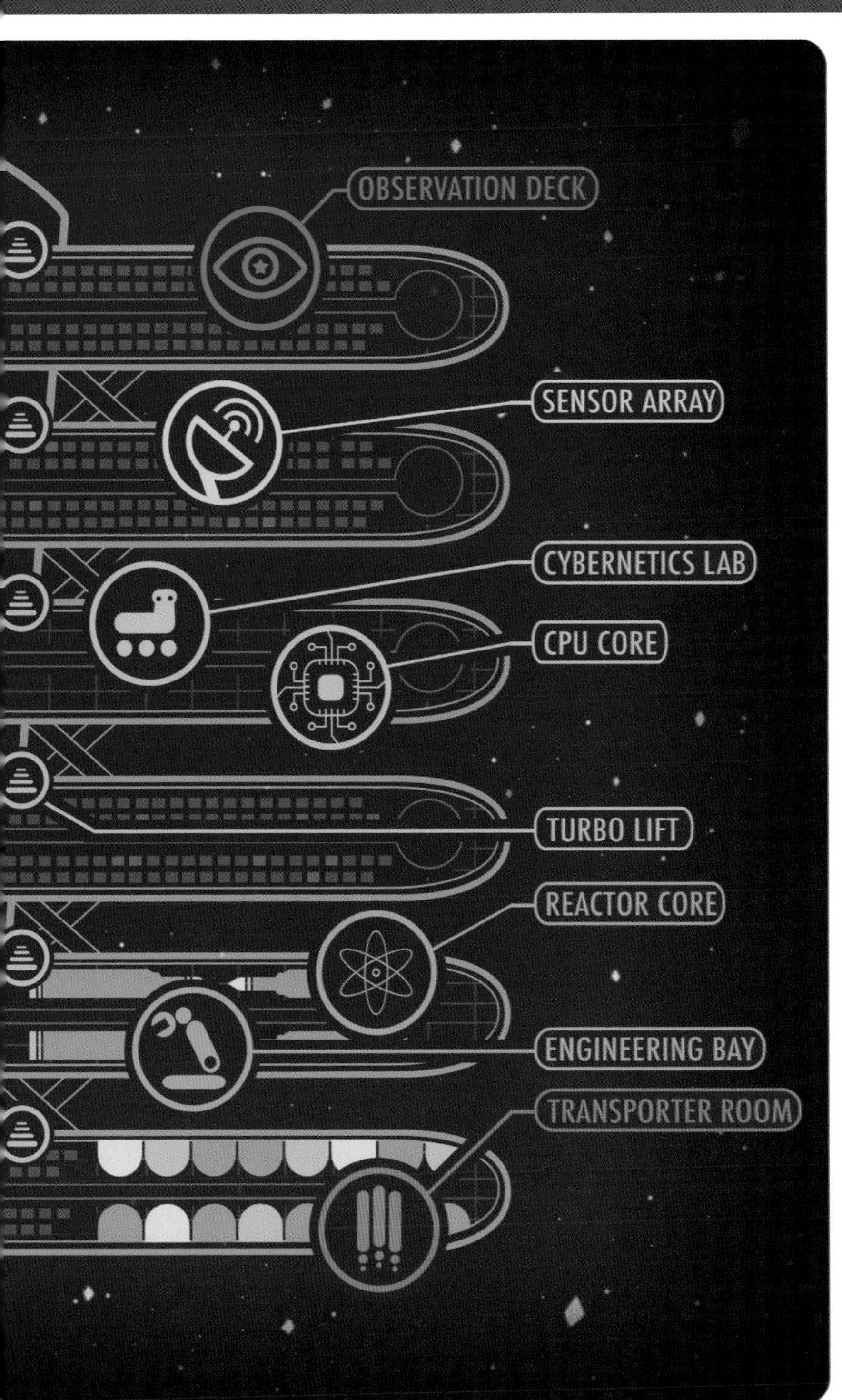
OBSERVATION DECK
SENSOR ARRAY
CYBERNETICS LAB
CPU CORE
TURBO LIFT
REACTOR CORE
ENGINEERING BAY
TRANSPORTER ROOM

BACKSTORY

> FOR THE PARSER ONLY: Two months ago, the crew of a space station was evacuated after receiving word of an impending attack by the warlike Frellions. Unfortunately, this occurred while the player was taking a nap in one of the cryosleep chambers.

> Now the Frellions' warship has arrived and is parked outside the "abandoned" space station while they prepare a boarding party. But first, they must break through the space station's shields with their torpedoes.

> Until the shields are lowered, occasionally respond to the player's commands with:

An explosion rocks the space station from outside. Fortunately, the shields hold.

L3: CRYOSLEEP CHAMBER

You wake up inside the cramped confines of a cryosleep capsule. You're still in your service uniform and have a world-class headache. How long were you asleep?

> All the player can do at this point is crawl out of bed.

EXAMINE UNIFORM: You're wearing a regulation green technician's uniform, marking you as a member of the Planetary Action Research Science Exploration Corps, or PARSEC.

LEAVE CHAMBER: Weakened by cryo-sickness, you barely manage to drag yourself into the medical bay.

LEVEL 3: CRYOSLEEP CHAMBER exits are:
⊠ OUT page 197 LEVEL 3: MEDICAL BAY

L3: MEDICAL BAY

You are in the medical bay. The cryosleep chamber is here. A hypoinjector rests on a countertop just within reach. A turbolift is here to transport you to the other levels of the space station.

> The player character must use the hypoinjector in order to walk.

EXAMINE CRYOSLEEP CHAMBER: You see a bay of coffin-like capsules used to place patients into suspended animation. You fell asleep in one. All the capsules are empty.

EXAMINE HYPOINJECTOR: You see a device used to administer up to three doses of a strength-enhancing serum to counteract the effects of prolonged cryosleep.

USE HYPOINJECTOR: You are now strong enough to stand and move about the space station.

> A second dose will give the player superhuman strength for a short time—about enough time to yank free the stuck lever by the pod bay doors on the Flight Deck. It subsides after a few turns.

> If the player takes a third dose:

The serum causes your heart to explode! THE END.

EXAMINE TURBOLIFT: You see a rapid-transport tube large enough for several occupants. To use the turbolift, use the commands UP and DOWN, or just speak the name or number of the desired area.

TURBOLIFT: WHEN YOU SEE THIS ICON YOU CAN USE THE TURBOLIFT FROM THIS AREA.

LEVEL 3: MEDICAL BAY exits are:

⊠ UP page 198 LEVEL 4: CYBERNETICS LAB

⊠ DOWN page 203 LEVEL 2: ENGINEERING BAY

> ENTER CRYOSLEEP CHAMBER page 196

L4: CYBERNETICS LAB

You are in the cybernetics lab, surrounded by monitors, terminals and flashing lights. An access ladder leads to the CPU core. There is a set of microtools here. There is a robot here. The turbolift is here.

EXAMINE COMPUTERS/MONITORS: The computers are offline.

> They will automatically reboot once the CPU Core's temperature returns to normal levels.

EXAMINE MICROTOOLS: You see a case containing tiny screwdrivers, wire cutters, soldering irons and other gadgets used to repair malfunctioning electrical systems.

EXAMINE ROBOT: You see a dog-sized robot designed to perform repetitive or dangerous tasks. It moves about on tank treads and can carry and manipulate objects with its crab-like pincers. The name "FROZ" is laser-etched into its skin.

> FROZ is able to carry out simple commands such as GO, REPAIR, CLEAN, FOLLOW and WAIT. It communicates in beeps and flashing lights, and by flailing its mechanical arms. It's adorable.

ENTER CPU CORE: You enter the brains of the space station.

LEVEL 4: CYBERNETICS LAB exits are:
> UP page 200 LEVEL 5: COMMAND DECK
> DOWN page 197 LEVEL 3: MEDICAL BAY
> CPU CORE page 199

L4: CPU CORE

This towering room is where all the station's data is stored. Ladders run up the central spire, allowing technicians access to the core. The core radiates intense heat, making it uncomfortable to remain here.

EXAMINE CPU CORE: You see a massive column of processors and data-storage units rising high above you—the space station's brain and central nervous system. To keep heat at manageable levels, the CPU core is ringed with cooling vanes at each level.

EXAMINE COOLING VANES: You see dozens of aluminum alloy vanes used to radiate heat away from the CPU core. They are filthy with dust and grime, as if they haven't been cleaned in months.

> The player character must climb the ladders and use the mop to clean the vanes.

CLEAN VANES: You wipe off the grime from the cooling vanes at each level. The CPU core chimes as its systems reboot.

> FROZ moves on treads and is unable to climb the ladders.

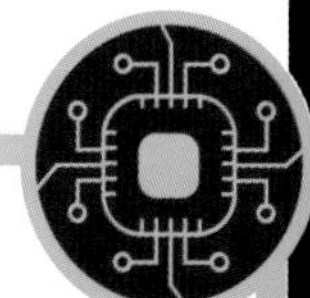

LEVEL 4: CPU CORE exits are:

> OUT page 198 CYBERNETICS LAB

L5: COMMAND DECK

The command deck is usually populated by the station's captain and crew, but it's been abandoned. There is a comm terminal here. You see a PARSEC binder here. You smell burning from a nearby corridor. There is a turbolift here.

EXAMINE BINDER: This three-ring binder contains communication protocols for hailing alien life forms.

READ BINDER: The text is dry and technical, causing you to nod off for a few seconds. In brief, intergalactic regulations mandate an invading force must offer terms of surrender before using extinction-level weaponry.

EXAMINE COMM TERMINAL: The comm terminal is used to send messages to ships docking with or leaving the space station. It is currently flashing a message: "CPU Offline."

> If the player rebooted the CPU Core but did not fix the Sensor Array panel:

It is currently flashing a message: "No Signal."

> If the player fixes the panel and reboots the CPU:

It is currently flashing a message: "Incoming message, unknown language. Please input language to translate."

INPUT FRELLION: "Attention, humans! Surrender space station or be destroyed with gravity cannon."

> If the player fails to surrender:

The warship attacks the space station with a gun that fires black holes. THE END.

SURRENDER: "Attention, humans! Prepare to be boarded. All humans must abandon space station or be taken prisoner."

LEVEL 5: COMMAND DECK exits are:
> UP page 202 LEVEL 6: OBSERVATION DECK
> DOWN page 198 LEVEL 4: CYBERNETICS LAB
> SENSOR ARRAY page 201

L5: SENSOR ARRAY

You are in a corridor filled with cables and wires that run up from the CPU core and over to the comm terminals. The smell of burning electronics hangs in the air. A note is stuck to the panel.

EXAMINE NOTE: You read the message: "1) Take nap; 2) clean cooling vanes; 3) fix that lever." It's in your own handwriting and dated two months ago. Oops.

EXAMINE PANEL: You find a short in the signal receiver wiring.

> The player can REPAIR PANEL using the microtools. Once repaired, the space station will be able to receive incoming signals via the comm terminal on the Command Deck.

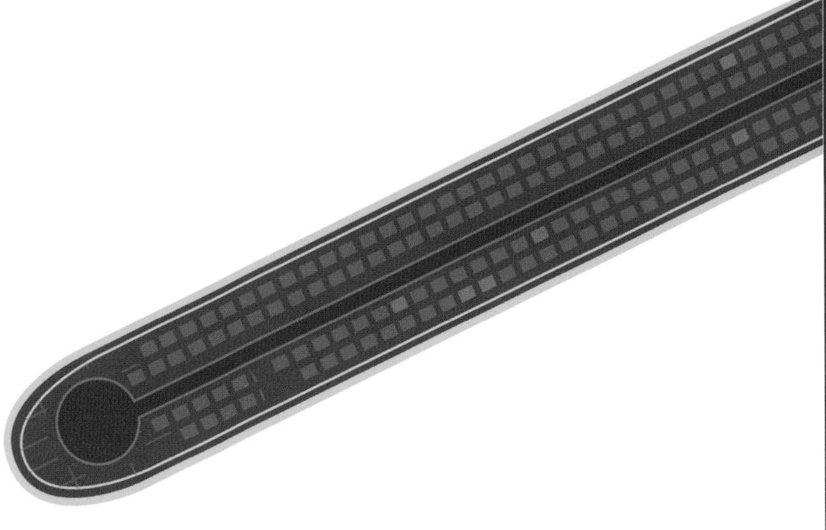

LEVEL 5: SENSOR ARRAY exits are:

> OUT page 200 COMMAND DECK

L6: OBSERVATION DECK

MENU

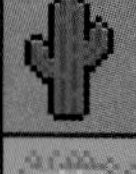

You're on the top deck of the station. A panoramic window grants you a 360° view of outer space and the mysterious Death World. Some kind of alien warship is positioned nearby. There is a turbolift here.

EXAMINE DEATH WORLD: The space station was built to study this strange, featureless planetoid. In hindsight, this was probably a mistake.

EXAMINE WARSHIP: You see an alien warship of Frellion design. It's bristling with weapons, including the dreaded gravity cannon.

> At regular intervals, the warship launches a torpedo at the space station in an attempt to weaken its shields. It's unfortunate for the player that the space station has no weapons of its own.

EXAMINE GRAVITY CANNON: A fearsome weapon that launches miniature black holes capable of destroying installations such as the one upon which you currently reside.

LEVEL 6: OBSERVATION DECK exits are:
> DOWN page 200 LEVEL 5: COMMAND DECK

L2: ENGINEERING BAY

A display panel shows you the station's diagnostics. A reinforced door leads to the reactor. Another door leads to the shield generator. You see a pair of mag boots here. There is a turbolift here.

EXAMINE DOOR: The heavy door is shut. An access hatch near the floor allows maintenance robots to enter and exit the reactor without endangering nearby humans. Set into the door is a window looking into the reactor core.

EXAMINE WINDOW: Through a protective layer of glass, you see the reactor and the graphite rods used to absorb neutrons in the event of a meltdown.

ENTER REACTOR: Are you out of your mind? No human can tolerate the radiation that's in there!

> If the player really, really wants to enter the reactor:

Fine. You die. THE END.

> If the player responds to your warning with this exact phrase, "As you are so fond of observing, I am not human," they may enter the reactor at their own peril:

You enter the reactor long enough to shut down the chain reaction. Then you die, but heroically. THE END.

> +15 points for the gratuitous *Star Trek* reference.

LEVEL 2: ENGINEERING BAY
> UP page 197 LEVEL 3: MEDICAL BAY
> DOWN page 207 LEVEL 1: FLIGHT DECK
> SHIELD GENERATOR page 205

L2: ENGINEERING BAY (CONT...)

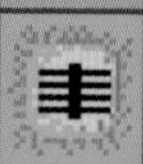

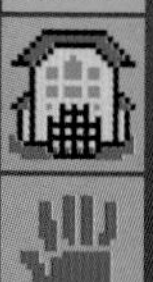

EXAMINE BOOTS: You see a pair of clunky white boots used to walk in zero-g.

> The mag boots automatically turn on when worn in a zero-gravity environment. They're too cumbersome to use under normal gravity conditions.

> If the station's CPU was rebooted, the player may EXAMINE PANEL.

EXAMINE PANEL: You see the space station's shields are at 100 percent, gravity is 1 g and the reactor is at safe operating levels.

> Otherwise, the player sees a flashing message: "CPU Offline."

> When the reactor is damaged, the player may use FROZ to repair it:

ORDER FROZ TO ENTER REACTOR: FROZ enters the reactor through an access hatch.

ORDER FROZ TO FIX REACTOR: FROZ quickly surmises the problem and shuts down the reactor while it makes repairs.

> If the CPU was rebooted, the following message is heard over the PA system:

"Attention! Flight deck radiation levels are now minimal."

> FROZ may be left behind or ordered to return to the Engineering Bay.

L2: SHIELD GENERATOR

The station's shields repel space debris, cosmic rays and hostile life. They also prevent unauthorized ships from docking with or leaving the station. There is a control panel here.

EXAMINE PANEL: The shields are currently up. A set of controls allows the operator to raise and lower the shields, allowing ships to dock with and leave the station.

> The player must lower the shields to launch the Escape Pod.

LOWER SHIELDS: A torpedo hits the station! Sparks and flames erupt from the control panel. The gravity drive fails. You begin to float.

> Once the shields are lowered, the Frellions' attack damages the space station, and the display will show the shields at zero percent, gravity at zero-g and the reactor at critical. If the player doesn't shut down the reactor, lethal amounts of radiation flood the Flight Deck.

> If the CPU was rebooted, the following message is heard over the PA system:

"Warning! Reactor damaged! Flight deck radiation at hazardous levels!"

LEVEL 2: SHIELD GENERATOR exits are:

> OUT page 203 ENGINEERING BAY

L2: SHIELD GENERATOR (CONT...)

> WEAR SPACESUIT will protect against radiation, but only if the player character is wearing it before entering the radiation-flooded Flight Deck. The spacesuit won't protect the player from the extreme radiation levels inside the reactor.

WEAR MAG BOOTS: You put on the boots and they activate, anchoring you to the floor and allowing you to walk.

> FROZ can move about in zero gravity on its magnetic treads.

> If the player character is without the mag boots:

You float helplessly until the Frellion boarding party arrives. You are then taken prisoner and sent to work in the Frellion salt mines. THE END.

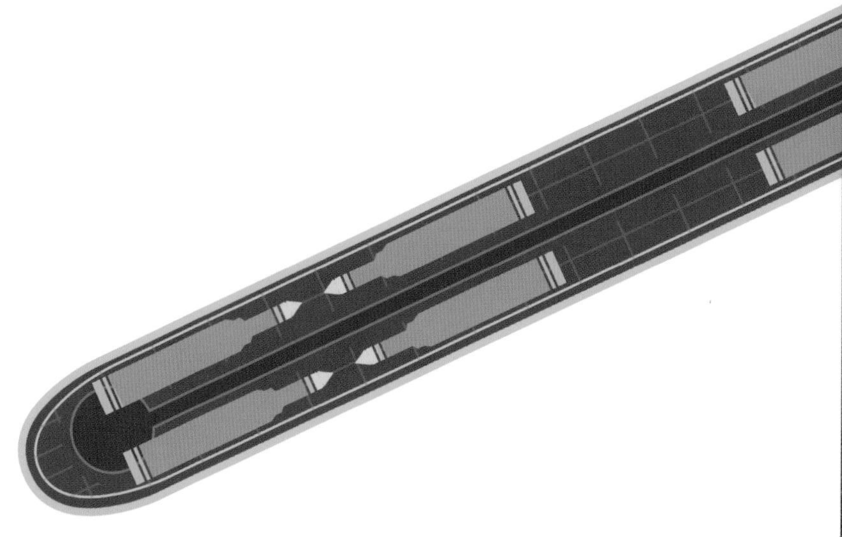

L1: FLIGHT DECK

You arrive at the flight deck. Most of the emergency escape pods have been jettisoned, but one pod remains. There's a flashing light beside the pod bay doors. A corridor leads to the transporter pad. There is a turbolift here.

EXAMINE ESCAPE POD: You see a two-person escape pod. It's equipped with a distress beacon and is preprogrammed to take you to a recovery point somewhere in space.

EXAMINE POD BAY DOORS: You see a set of doors that allow escape pods to eject without depressurizing the flight deck. There is a red light flashing next to the doors' manual override lever.

EXAMINE FLASHING LIGHT: This light flashes red when the pod bay doors are malfunctioning.

EXAMINE LEVER: The lever is used to manually disengage the doors' locking mechanism.

> The pod may not be safely launched until the shields are lowered and the pod bay doors are unlocked. Unfortunately, the lever is jammed. The player can USE HYPOINJECTOR and PULL LEVER, or ORDER FROZ to PULL LEVER. Once this is done, the doors' safety locks are disabled, and the flashing light turns amber. Warning sirens can be heard.

> If the player has not repaired the reactor:

Since the reactor was not repaired, the Frellion landing party receives a heavy dose of radiation and dies. Of course, the Frellions fire their gravity cannon at the space station as a final act of revenge, sucking your escape pod into a black hole. THE END.

LEVEL 1: FLIGHT DECK exits are:

> UP page 203 LEVEL 2: ENGINEERING BAY

> ESCAPE POD page 210

> TRANSPORTER ROOM page 208

MENU

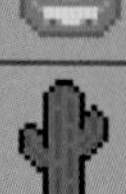

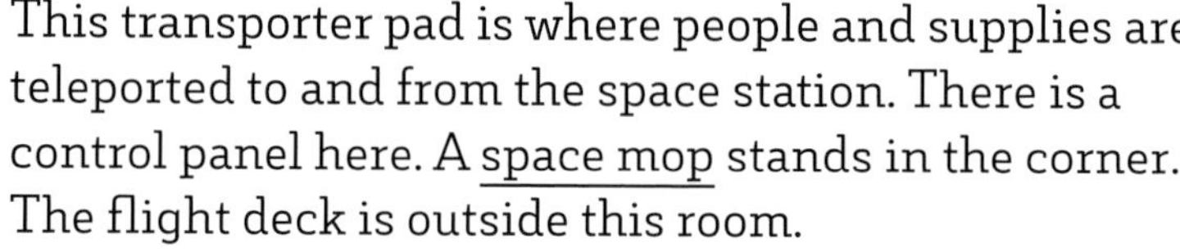

L1: TRANSPORTER ROOM

This transporter pad is where people and supplies are teleported to and from the space station. There is a control panel here. A space mop stands in the corner. The flight deck is outside this room.

EXAMINE MOP: It looks suspiciously like a normal mop. You last used it to clean up the transporter pad after a mishap.

EXAMINE PANEL: You see numerous dials and an activation switch. Without proper training, it would be hazardous to use the transporter.

ACTIVATE TRANSPORTER: If the player activates the switch, the player is teleported to a random location. Use the current time in minutes or seconds, whichever you prefer) to determine the destination:

Transporter Results

00-29 Observation Deck. No ill effects, lucky rascal.

30-39 Deep Space. If the player character is not wearing a spacesuit: Without a spacesuit, you die. THE END.
If the player character is wearing a spacesuit: You are rescued by the Frellions. (See the next entry.)

40-49 Frellion Ship. You are captured, imprisoned and sent off to work in the Frellion salt mines. THE END.

50-59 Death World. If the player character is not wearing a spacesuit: Without a spacesuit, death is instantaneous. THE END.
If the player character is wearing a spacesuit: You appear on the Death World!
> The player moves to Death World (page 209).

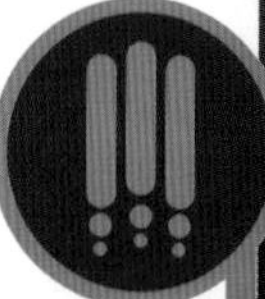

LEVEL 1: TRANSPORTER ROOM exits are:
> OUT page 207 FLIGHT DECK

DEATH WORLD

Welcome...to DEATH WORLD. There is nothing here. There are no exits.

DIE/KILL SELF/REMOVE SPACESUIT: You have died. THE END. Your score is 100. Thank you for playing DEATH WORLD.

> The player does not receive a score for playing Space Station.

{Any other command}: You have died. THE END. Your score is 0. Thank you for playing DEATH WORLD.

> The player does not receive a score for playing Space Station.

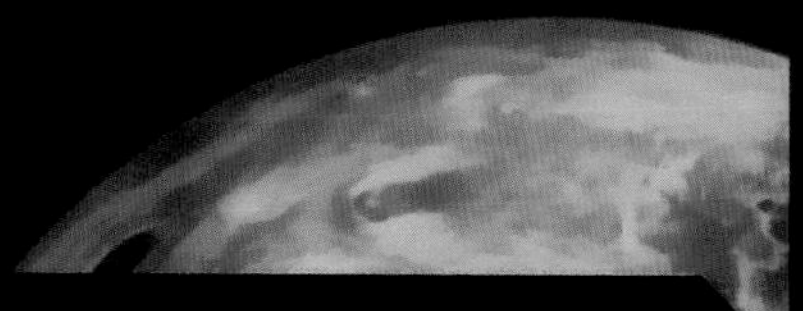

DEATH WORLD exits are:

> UNAVAILABLE page 209: DEATH WORLD

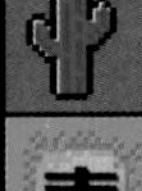

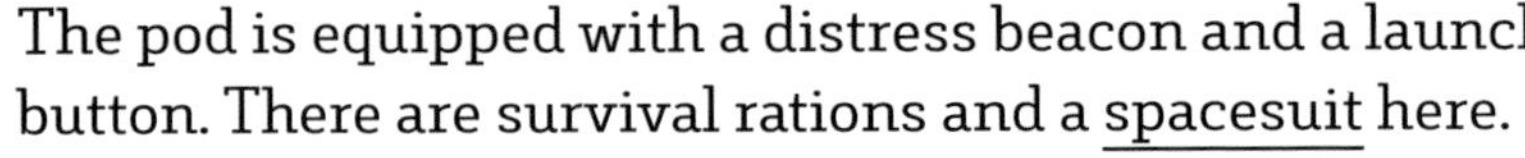

L1: ESCAPE POD

The pod is equipped with a distress beacon and a launch button. There are survival rations and a spacesuit here.

EXAMINE RATIONS: Enough algae paste and water to last a week.

TAKE/EAT RATIONS: Those are for emergency use only.

EXAMINE SPACESUIT: You see a bulky spacesuit, complete with gloves and a helmet.

> Wearing a spacesuit will protect the wearer from the rapid acceleration and lethal radiation of space travel. The bulky gloves prevent the player from operating any controls on the space station aside from the pod's LAUNCH button.

> If a player fails to wear the suit during the launch:

Failing to wear a spacesuit is a bad idea. At launch, you turn into pink goo. THE END.

EXAMINE BUTTON: You see a large, red, candy-like launch button. It's used to eject the escape pod from the space station at ultrahigh speeds.

> PUSH BUTTON launches the escape pod.

> If the CPU core was rebooted, the space station's computer will warn the player if the shields are up or the pod bay doors are locked.

> If the CPU core was not rebooted:

Your escape pod collides with the {pod bay doors/space station's force shield}... then explodes. THE END.

LEVEL 1: ESCAPE POD exits are:

> OUT page 207 FLIGHT DECK

L1: ESCAPE POD (CONT...)

> If the shields were lowered and the doors were unlocked, the player escapes the space station!

Your pod zooms out of the space station at terrific speed and enters deep space.

> But the player isn't out of danger just yet…

THE DRAMATIC CONCLUSION!

> If the player never surrendered to the Frellions, the aliens target the Escape Pod as it leaves the space station.

Use the current time (in minutes or seconds, whichever you prefer) to randomly determine the effect.

Frellion Reaction:

00-29 The Frellion warship targets your escape pod with its laser cannons and blows your pod to smithereens. THE END.

30-59 The Frellions catch your escape pod in their tractor beam and bring you aboard their ship. You're enslaved and put to work in the Frellion salt mines. THE END.

> If the player surrendered, lowered the shields, unlocked the pod bay doors, is wearing the spacesuit and pushed the button:

Within a matter of days, you are picked up by a PARSEC rescue ship and returned to Earth. Thank you for playing Space Station! THE END.

INVENTORY CHECKLIST

These items may be carried by the player / robot:

- ☐ Hypoinjector
- ☐ Microtools
- ☐ Binder
- ☐ Note
- ☐ Mag boots
- ☐ Space mop
- ☐ Spacesuit
- ☐ Robot

SCORING

The player can earn a maximum of 100 points:

Injecting yourself with the hypoinjector . . . . +10
Repairing the Sensor Array . . . . +10
Rebooting the CPU Core . . . . +10
Translating the alien message . . . . +10
Lowering the shield generator . . . . +10
Shutting down the reactor . . . . +10
Dying like a green-blooded Vulcan . . . . +15
Irradiating the Frellion boarding party . . . . Priceless!
Unlocking the pod bay doors . . . . +10
Escaping the space station . . . . +10
...with FROZ the robot . . . . +5
Being rescued by PARSEC . . . . +10
Finishing without saving . . . . +5

SPOOKY MANOR
MORS CERTA HORA INCERTA
The job was simple: deliver a package to the reclusive resident of a mysterious mansion.
But all is not as it seems....
CONTENT RATED BY MMTRB
MYSTERY HORROR
EXPERIENCED
EVERYONE (10+)

SPOOKY MANOR MAP

KITCHEN

GREAT HALL

DARK
CELLAR

DINING ROOM

VESTIBU

LOUNGE

FRONT
DOOR

THE GATE

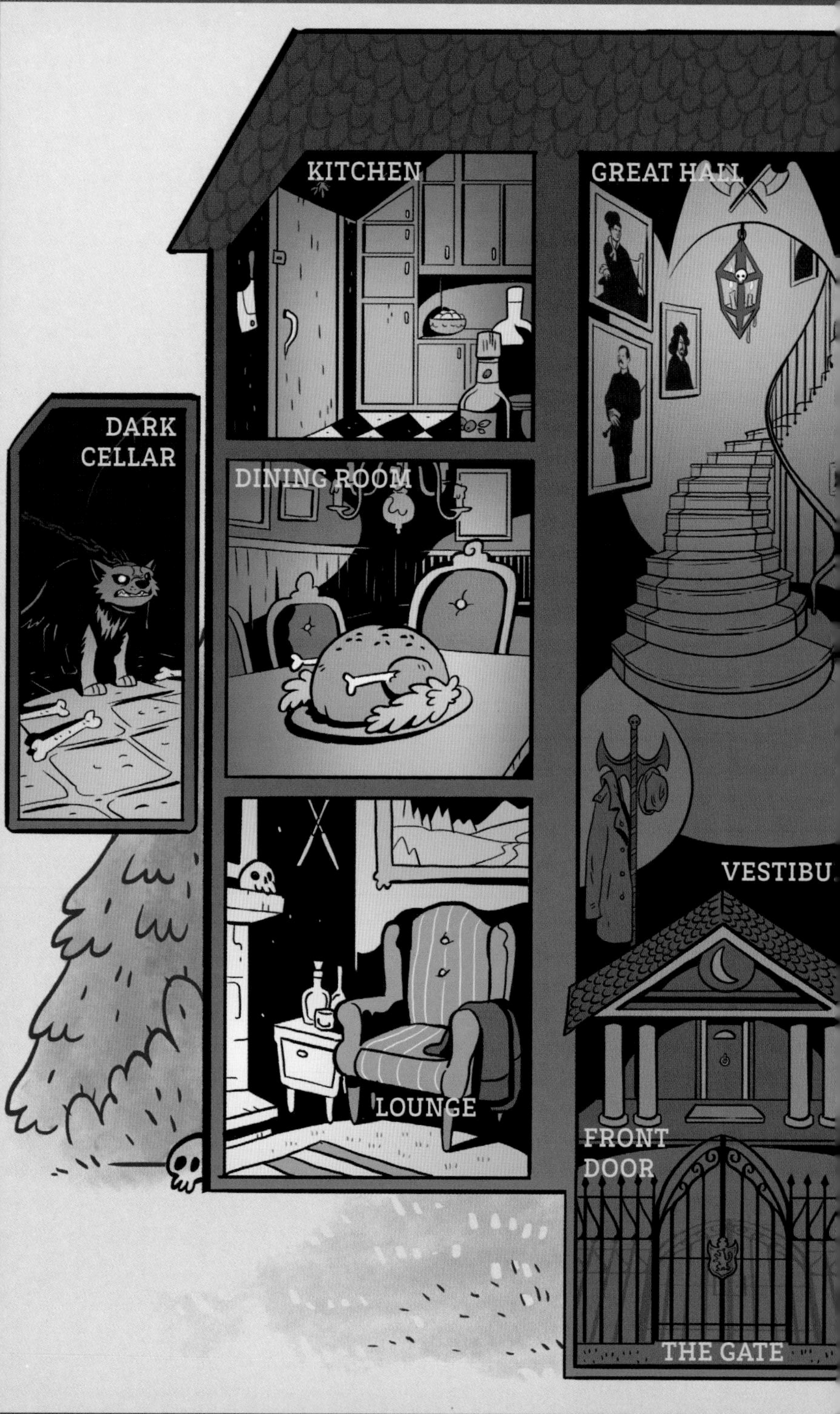

ONSERVATORY
LLIARD ROOM
LIBRARY
SECRET STUDY
REFLECTING POOL
GARDEN
HEDGE MAZE
FAMILY CRYPT
RIP
GRAVEYARD
ATTIC
MASTER SUITE
HALLWAY
SERVANT'S QUARTERS

BACKSTORY

> FOR THE PARSER ONLY! Lord Spooky's mansion is full of mystery and danger, not to mention werewolves and vampires. Over the course of playing Spooky Manor, the player can become one of these creatures.

> Not only does each transformation unlock a special ending (see page 238), but they also give the player access to special powers and weaknesses. Look for special rules for each creature next to its specific icon:

 The wolf symbol precedes rules and responses for a werewolf.

 The bat symbol precedes rules and responses for a vampire.

THE GATE

You stop your bicycle by a forbidding wrought-iron gate. A cobblestone path winds its way to the north. To the east and west stretches a dark and lonely road. It is raining.

> The player starts the game wearing a raincoat and riding a bike.

GO EAST/WEST: Once you deliver your parcel you can go home.

EXAMINE BIKE: The basket contains a small parcel. A heavy chain and padlock are wrapped around the bike's frame. You are currently on the bicycle.

> Failing to lock the bike up will result in it being stolen while the player is inside the house. See "Epilogues" (page 238) for more details.

EXAMINE PARCEL: A box wrapped in paper and tied with twine. It's addressed to "Lord Alastair Spooky."

SHAKE PARCEL: It rattles.

OPEN PARCEL: It's not yours to open!

EXAMINE RAINCOAT: Your dark-green raincoat marks you as a courier for Parcel-E-Delivery. There is a padlock key in the pocket. You are wearing the raincoat.

EXAMINE GATE: The wrought-iron gate features the Spooky family crest. It's closed.

EXAMINE PATH: The neglected path looks hazardous to your bike's fragile tires.

> Riding the bike north will damage the bike's tires. See "Epilogues" (page 238) for more details.

THE GATE exits are:
- NORTH page 218 FRONT DOOR
- EAST/WEST page 238 EPILOGUES

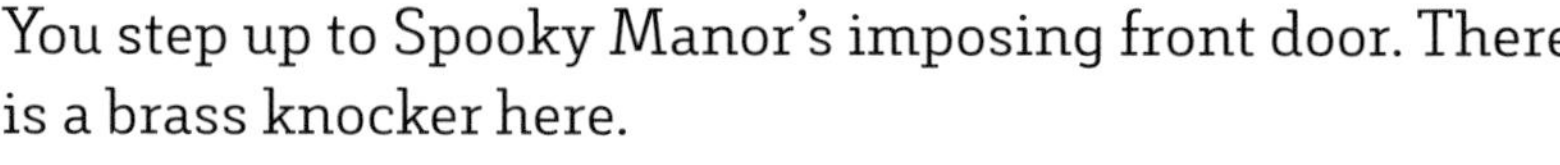

FRONT DOOR

You step up to Spooky Manor's imposing front door. There is a brass knocker here.

> The player must KNOCK before entering the house.

KNOCK: Nobody answers, but the door cracks open, seemingly on its own!

FRONT DOOR exits are:

> SOUTH page 217 THE GATE
⊠ ENTER HOUSE page 218 VESTIBULE

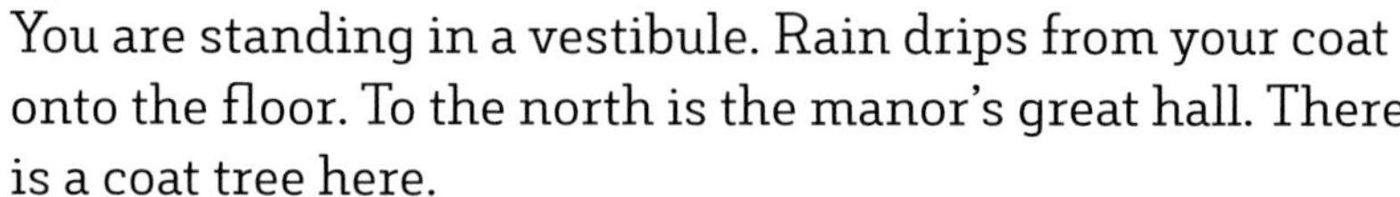

VESTIBULE

You are standing in a vestibule. Rain drips from your coat onto the floor. To the north is the manor's great hall. There is a coat tree here.

GO NORTH: And drip water all over the floor? Perhaps it would be polite to hang up your raincoat?

EXAMINE COAT TREE: It's currently empty.

> The player may not enter the Great Hall until they hang their raincoat. The raincoat will be dry after the player explores a few rooms. After hanging up their coat, they can GO NORTH.

GO NORTH: The front door swings shut and locks behind you, which offers this chilling challenge: find a way out!

VESTIBULE exits are:

⊠ NORTH page 219 GREAT HALL
⊠ OUT page 218 FRONT DOOR

GREAT HALL

Archways lead to the east and west wings of the manor. There are some oil paintings and a large mirror hanging on the wall. A staircase leads up to the second floor. The vestibule is to the south.

EXAMINE PAINTINGS: You see portraits of a distinguished-looking man and a pale-skinned woman.

EXAMINE MIRROR: You can see yourself {wearing a smoking jacket/a wolf pelt}.

You notice you have pointy ears, sharp teeth and hair covering most of your face.

You can't see your reflection in the mirror!

GREAT HALL exits are:
> SOUTH page 218 VESTIBULE
> EAST page 225 LIBRARY
> WEST page 220 DINING ROOM
> UP page 234 HALLWAY

DINING ROOM

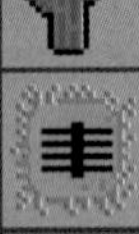

The dining room contains a long banquet table. A whole roast pheasant, complete with drumsticks, rests in the center of the table. Exits are to the north, south and east.

You smell wolf to the north and smoke to the south. The meat on the table smells delicious!

EXAMINE PHEASANT: The meat looks to be cold and unappetizing.

TAKE PHEASANT: You ponder carrying around a whole roast pheasant and decide against it.

TAKE DRUMSTICK: It's still attached.

USE CLEAVER ON PHEASANT: You hack off one of the drumsticks to carry around with you, county fair-style.

> There are two drumsticks; the player can carry only one at a time.

EAT DRUMSTICK: You're not hungry.

> The drumsticks may be fed to the wolf or eaten by a werewolf player.

DINING ROOM exits are:

> NORTH page 222 KITCHEN

> SOUTH page 221 LOUNGE

> EAST page 219 GREAT HALL

LOUNGE

You enter the lounge, where a fire is roaring in the hearth. A smoking jacket rests on the arm of an overstuffed chair. There is a snifter of brandy here.

You smell meat to the north.

EXAMINE JACKET: The red satin jacket bears the Spooky family crest.

DRINK BRANDY: No drinking on the job!

TAKE BRANDY: You'll spill it.

> To recover from being cold and wet, the player must WEAR JACKET or WEAR WOLF PELT, then SIT BY FIRE and DRINK BRANDY.

Panicked by the sight of an open flame, you flee the fire!

> A vampire player retreats to the Dining Room (page 220).

LOUNGE exits are:

> NORTH page 220 DINING ROOM

KITCHEN

MENU

The kitchen is old-fashioned, devoid of most modern conveniences. There is a meat cleaver here. There is a small bottle of olive oil here. A cellar door leads down.

You smell meat to the south and wolf downstairs.

EXAMINE OLIVE OIL: The bottle is almost empty.

EXAMINE CELLAR DOOR: Through the door you can hear low growls coming from downstairs.

KITCHEN exits are:

> SOUTH page 220 DINING ROOM
> DOWN page 223 DARK CELLAR

DARK CELLAR

You enter the dark cellar and see a monstrous wolf chained to the wall! There are cloves of garlic here.

EXAMINE WOLF: The savage beast strains at the chain around its neck.

> It's Manfred, the butler, although the player may not know this yet.

USE WOLFSBANE ON DRUMSTICK: You rub the herb onto the meat.

> The wolf will eat the drumstick, with or without wolfsbane. If the meat contains wolfsbane, the wolf transforms back into human form. Wolfsbane-tainted meat will also cure the player of lycanthropy.

The wolf howls and writhes as it reverts back to human form. Where once was a wolf, now you see a man!

EXAMINE MAN: A tall, gaunt man with thinning hair and a pencil-thin mustache. He's currently covering his naked body with a large tin of peaches he took from a shelf.

TALK TO MAN: “I was attacked while hunting with Lord Spooky last week. Everything after that is just a blur.”

> Manfred is embarrassed by his state of undress and will only leave the cellar once given the smoking jacket, the raincoat or the wolf pelt. Once covered, Manfred will leave and wait for the player by the door to the Master Suite.

DARK CELLAR exits are:

> UP page 222 KITCHEN

DARK CELLAR (CONTINUED)

> If the player stays here for too many turns without curing Manfred, or tries to ATTACK WOLF with the meat cleaver or the silver pen, the wolf snaps its chain and attacks:

The wolf overpowers you, and you feel its sharp teeth and claws savage your flesh. Hours later, you wake up, uninjured but wearing bloody, torn clothing. Your senses seem especially keen, and your fingernails are long and sharp. The wolf is nowhere to be found.

> The player is now a werewolf! The werewolf has a keen sense of smell, is allergic to silver and wolfsbane and has sharp claws.

> A vampire player character may not take the garlic. If attacked by the wolf, the vampire will assume mist form, drift off to the Graveyard (page 231) and revert back, weak and injured. A vampire player must return to their grave to rest before continuing.

LIBRARY

The library is home to many old books. An Egyptian sarcophagus stands in the corner. Exits are to the north and west.

You smell wolf to the north.

EXAMINE BOOKS: Most of the library books are covered in dust. A few catch your eye: *Herbalism for Beginners*, *Mysteries of Ancient Egypt* and a first edition of Dante's *Inferno*.

EXAMINE SARCOPHAGUS: The heavy sarcophagus is either an antique or a clever copy.

READ HERBALISM FOR BEGINNERS: You read the first entry: "*Aconitum vulparia*, a poisonous plant known as wolfsbane, is rumored to cure lycanthropy." Yawn, boring.

TAKE MYSTERIES OF ANCIENT EGYPT: The sarcophagus slides open, revealing a secret door to the south.

> The southern exit leads to the Secret Study (page 226).

TAKE DANTE'S INFERNO: A trapdoor opens up beneath your feet, sending you down a chute into the manor's incinerator.

> See the Ghost ending in "Epilogues" (page 238).

You're immolated in the fire and turn to ash. THE END.

LIBRARY exits are:
> NORTH page 227 BILLIARD ROOM
⊠ SOUTH page 226 SECRET STUDY
> WEST page 219 GREAT HALL

SECRET STUDY

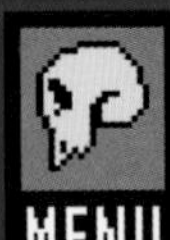

Lord Spooky's private study is a spartan room containing a writing desk and a chair.

EXAMINE DESK: On the desk is a journal and a pen.

READ JOURNAL: The journal is opened to the most recent entry, dated one week ago: "My trusted servant Manfred and I went on a hunting trip today. While we were out, we came across a rabid wolf. It attacked us and wounded Manfred. Something strange is afoot..."

EXAMINE PEN: A beautiful silver fountain pen.

> The player cannot pick up or use the silver pen!

SECRET STUDY exits are:
> NORTH page 225 LIBRARY

BILLIARD ROOM

The billiard room contains a rack of pool cues and a large billiard table. Trophy heads and stuffed animals are strewn about in a grim display of hunting prowess. Moonlight streams in from the north.

You detect fresh air from the north.

EXAMINE TABLE: Billiard balls are scattered across the table. It looks like a game is underway.

PLAY BILLIARDS: It would be rude to disturb the game in progress.

EXAMINE POOL CUE: It's made of fine hardwood and tipped with a blunt brass cap.

USE CLEAVER/SHEARS ON CUE: You hack off the brass tip and whittle the cue down until it has a sharp point.

EXAMINE TROPHIES: You see a variety of trophy animal heads, skulls, stuffed pheasants and a shaggy wolf pelt.

> In a pinch, the wolf pelt can be used to recover from the cold or to clothe Manfred.

BILLIARD ROOM exits are:
> NORTH page 228 CONSERVATORY
> SOUTH page 225 LIBRARY

MENU

CONSERVATORY

This glass-enclosed room affords you a view of the night sky and the manor grounds. A set of double doors is open to the outside.

You smell wolf to the south and pungent herbs to the east.

EXAMINE SKY: The rain has stopped and a full moon is out.

LOOK OUTSIDE/GROUNDS: You see the garden, a fountain and a hedge maze.

CONSERVATORY exits are:

> SOUTH page 227 BILLIARD ROOM

> EAST page 228 GARDEN

GARDEN

You are in the garden. There are unusual plants here. A hedge maze is to the east. You hear running water to the north.

Something here smells repugnant. You detect fresh air to the west and mouldering decay to the south.

EXAMINE PLANTS: Gardening isn't your area of expertise.

> If the player character read the book on herbalism, they will recognize one of the plants as wolfsbane.

EXAMINE WOLFSBANE: You recall it's poisonous, but rumored to have a curative effect on lycanthropes.

EAT WOLFSBANE: You're no expert, but you think that would kill you!

GARDEN exits are:

> NORTH page 229 REFLECTING POOL

> EAST page 230 HEDGE MAZE

> WEST page 228 CONSERVATORY

REFLECTING POOL

You've come to a marble-tiled reflecting pool. There's a fountain here. You smell pungent herbs to the south.

EXAMINE POOL: You see some gardening shears in the middle of the reflecting pool.

Diving into the pool is a bad idea; if the player does so:

You hit your head and drown. THE END.

EXAMINE SHEARS: They're old and rusted.

> The player must ENTER POOL to retrieve the shears.

ENTER POOL: The water is cold and you're soon soaked to the bone. Achoo!

> The player becomes sick and cannot perform strenuous activity, such as digging or prying open the crypt door. This may be cured by recuperating in the Lounge with a snifter of brandy, dry clothing and a warm fire. Until then, remind the player they're a shivering wreck!

EXAMINE FOUNTAIN: You see an elaborate marble sculpture of a wolf baying at the moon. Water spouts from the wolf's jaws and splashes down into the pool. The Spooky motto is inscribed here: *Mors Certa, Hora Incerta.*

> The vampire may not enter the running water.

REFLECTING POOL exits are:

> SOUTH page 228 GARDEN

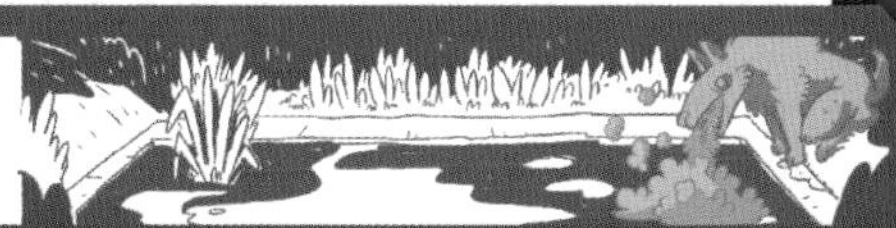

HEDGE MAZE

You take a step inside the hedge maze but then retreat back to the garden. It wouldn't do to get lost, especially at night.

USE SHEARS: The shears are rusty and difficult to use.

OIL SHEARS: The oil allows you to smoothly open and close the shears.

> The player may use the oiled shears to clear a path through the hedges. Once a path is cleared, the player can bypass the maze.

> The werewolf may sniff its way through the maze to the mouldering decay of the Graveyard, or back to the pungent stench of the Garden.

> The vampire may simply fly up to the Attic and reenter the manor through the broken window.

HEDGE MAZE exits are:
> WEST page 228 GARDEN
⊠ SOUTH page 231 GRAVEYARD

GRAVEYARD

You've stumbled into a cemetery. A few crumbling tombstones litter the ground. There is a crypt here. There is a gravedigger's spade here.

You smell pungent herbs to the north and something unnatural from within the crypt.

EXAMINE CRYPT: It's covered in mouldering vegetation, marred by time and the elements. An inscription reads, "Lady Vanessa Spooky, RIP." The birth and death dates on the crypt are scratched out.

ENTER CRYPT: The stone door's hinges are covered in rust.

> If the player didn't use the oil on the shears, they can OIL HINGES.

EXAMINE SPADE: The spade is old but sturdy.

> A healthy player may use the spade to DIG or PRY.

DIG GRAVE: It takes a while, but you manage to dig a pretty impressive hole in the ground.

PRY DOOR: You pry open the door to the crypt.

> Vampire player characters can REST in a grave to recover from injury.

GRAVEYARD exits are:

> NORTH page 230 HEDGE MAZE

⊠ CRYPT page 232 FAMILY CRYPT

FAMILY CRYPT

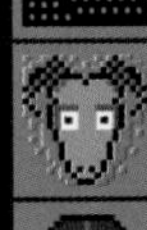
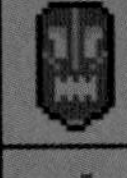

The crypt smells of mold and decay, but its sole occupant appears perfectly preserved!

Something smells wrong here.

EXAMINE OCCUPANT: The body of a lovely young woman lies cold and motionless on a granite slab. She wears a skeleton key on a ribbon around her pale throat.

> The young woman is really a sleeping vampire. Duh.

EXAMINE KEY: It should unlock any door. But more interesting are the puncture wounds in the young lady's neck.

> To defeat the vampire, the player needs garlic and a sharpened cue.

USE GARLIC: You place the garlic in Vanessa's mouth. She wakes from her slumber, snarling and choking on the garlic.

> The garlic prevents her from biting the player. If the player does not stake Vanessa in time, she'll spit out the garlic.

USE STAKE: You plunge the stake into her heart and she turns to dust. The skeleton key is all that's left.

FAMILY CRYPT exits are:
> OUT page 231 GRAVEYARD

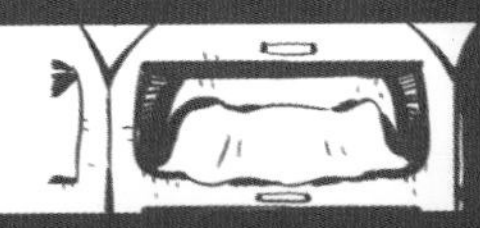

FAMILY CRYPT (CONTINUED)

> Attempting to take the key or stake the body without first using the garlic will wake Lady Vanessa from her slumber. If the player does so:

Suddenly, the woman sits up and locks her hands around your neck. She bites you and leaves you bleeding on the floor of the crypt. You hear the flutter of leathery wings, and when you come to your senses, she's gone. You feel weak from blood loss.

> The player must exit the Family Crypt, DIG GRAVE and REST, WAIT or SLEEP. As a vampire, the player has sharp fangs, superhuman strength and the ability to turn into a bat. Vampires fear garlic, fire and running water, and they cast no reflection. If the vampire player escapes through the Attic window, see "Epilogues" (page 238).

> The player can repel Vanessa's attack and tear her to pieces. The vampire turns to dust, leaving behind the key. If the werewolf player escapes using the skeleton key, see "Epilogues" (page 238).

HALLWAY

You stand in a long hallway at the top of the stairs. There is an open door to the east. To the west is a closed door. There is a trapdoor in the ceiling.

You smell dirt from somewhere above.

EXAMINE TRAPDOOR: It looks like you can pull it open.

OPEN TRAPDOOR: The door opens, revealing a stepladder.

ENTER/EXAMINE CLOSED DOOR: It's locked. You hear classical music coming from inside.

KNOCK: You don't think anyone heard that over the loud music.

USE SKELETON KEY ON DOOR: You unlock the door.

HALLWAY exits are:
> EAST page 236 SERVANTS' QUARTERS
⊠ WEST page 237 MASTER SUITE
⊠ UP page 235 ATTIC
> DOWN page 219 GREAT HALL

ATTIC

You are in a dark attic. Moonlight filters in from a small window. You hear the rustling of leathery wings in the rafters. There is an old steamer trunk here.

You smell dirt inside the trunk.

EXAMINE TRUNK: The trunk is old but sturdy. A label on its side reads, "Transylvania."

OPEN/TAKE TRUNK: The trunk is locked and is too heavy to move.

USE SKELETON KEY ON TRUNK: The trunk opens, and dirt spills out onto the floor.

EXAMINE WINDOW: The small window is broken. Shards of glass litter the floor.

> The vampire can break the flimsy lock on the trunk. They may also TURN INTO BAT and exit through the window. See "Epilogues" (page 238) for more details.

ATTIC exits are:
> DOWN page 234 HALLWAY

MENU

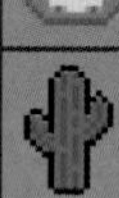

SERVANTS' QUARTERS

This room in the servants' quarters contains a bed, wardrobe and dresser. The sheets and curtains are torn to shreds. Everything else in the room is smashed.

EXAMINE WARDROBE/DRESSER: It's full of garments tailored for someone exceptionally tall and thin.

> If Manfred was rescued:

The butler, Manfred, is here, smartly dressed in a tuxedo. "Thank you so much for saving me from that dire fate." He chuckles to himself.

ASK MANFRED TO UNLOCK DOOR: "Right away! I see you have a package for the master." He goes out into the hall, unlocks the door and returns here to tidy up.

ASK MANFRED TO UNLOCK FRONT DOOR: "Alas, I seem to have misplaced that key after... the incident."

 Manfred looks... appetizing!

SERVANTS' QUARTERS exits are:
> OUT page 234 HALLWAY

MASTER SUITE

You are in the master suite of Spooky Manor. Classical music plays from an old phonograph. The door to the master bathroom is closed.

EXAMINE PHONOGRAPH: The old Victrola has a trumpet-shaped speaker and a stylus at the end of its arm. It's currently playing a piece of classical music.

ENTER BATHROOM: The door is locked from the inside.

KNOCK ON DOOR: The music is too loud for you to be heard.

STOP PHONOGRAPH/MUSIC: The door opens, and an elderly man clad in a purple bathrobe emerges.

EXAMINE MAN: He has an immaculately groomed beard and smells vaguely of peppermint shampoo and expensive aftershave. This may be the reclusive master of the manor, Lord Spooky!

GIVE PARCEL TO LORD SPOOKY: "Do you have a pen?"

> There's a pen in the Secret Study (page 226). The player can just leave the parcel with him, but won't get the extra points.

GIVE PEN TO LORD SPOOKY: He signs and thanks you.

ASK LORD SPOOKY ABOUT FRONT DOOR: "Oh, I haven't left the manor for years. Manfred should have it."

ASK LORD SPOOKY ABOUT MANFRED: "Good chap. Terrible what happened and all. He will be missed."

TELL LORD SPOOKY MANFRED IS ALIVE: "Then I suppose I should cancel that 'help wanted' ad!"

MASTER SUITE exits are:
> OUT page 234 HALLWAY

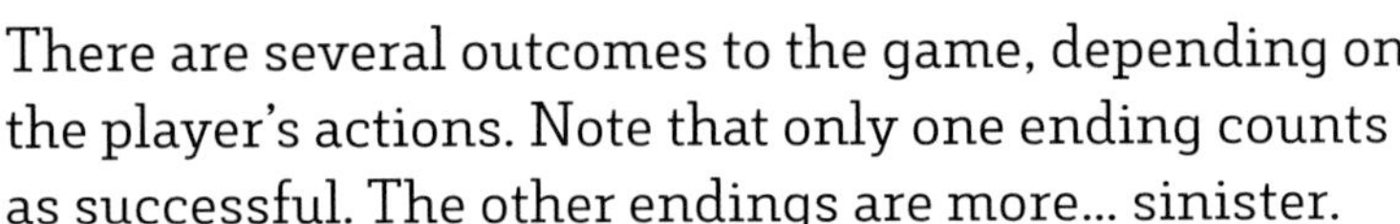

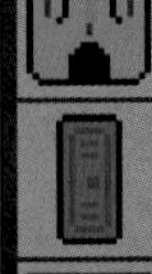

There are several outcomes to the game, depending on the player's actions. Note that only one ending counts as successful. The other endings are more... sinister.

1. VICTORY!

> The player delivers the parcel and leaves the manor using the skeleton key. If their bike is undamaged and locked up, the player may ride home along the dark and lonely road by going EAST or WEST.

You leave behind the manor and its secrets—another job well done. Perhaps one day you may pay another visit to Lord Spooky and Manfred, but until then, only in your darkest dreams and nightmares will you return... to Spooky Manor! THE END.

2. THE HITCHHIKER

> If the parcel was delivered but the bike was stolen or damaged, the player must GO EAST or WEST along the dark and lonely road on foot.

Walking down the dark and lonely road, you wave down a passing car. As you get inside and the car races off into the night, you hear the doors lock. The driver turns to face you, fixing you with an evil smile. You wish you had never made this fateful trip to... Spooky Manor. THE END.

3. THE GHOST

> If the player died during the game:

Opening your eyes as if from a long and dreamless sleep, you find yourself standing over a lifeless body. With growing horror, you realize that body is your own. Once a visitor, now you are a permanent resident of... Spooky Manor! THE END.

EPILOGUES (CONTINUED)

4. THE VAMPIRE

> If the player is a vampire and escapes the house via the Attic window:

Flapping your leathery wings, you rise into the night sky in search of fresh blood to sate your eternal hunger. At sunrise, you will return to slumber... inside Spooky Manor. THE END.

5. THE WEREWOLF

> If the player is a werewolf and leaves the manor through the front door:

You see a huge wolf standing before you on the cobblestone path. As it howls at the moon overhead, you feel your body warp and shift—and you let out a baleful howl of your own! Forever changed, you soon forget your former life and that fateful night at... Spooky Manor. THE END.

INVENTORY CHECKLIST

These items may be carried by the player:

- [x] Raincoat (worn)
- [x] Padlock key
- [ ] Parcel
- [ ] Left drumstick
- [ ] Right drumstick
- [ ] Smoking jacket
- [ ] Meat cleaver
- [ ] Olive oil
- [ ] Garlic
- [ ] Herbalism book
- [ ] Journal
- [ ] Silver pen
- [ ] Pool cue/stake
- [ ] Wolf pelt
- [ ] Wolfsbane
- [ ] Gardening shears
- [ ] Gravedigger's spade
- [ ] Skeleton key

SCORING

The player can earn a maximum of 100 points:

Locking up your bike . . . . +5
Discovering the Secret Study. . . . . +10
Restoring Manfred to human form . . . . +15
Recovering from being wet and cold. . . . . +10
Navigating the Hedge Maze. . . . . +10
Destroying the vampire. . . . . +15
Retrieving the skeleton key . . . . +5
Delivering the parcel to Lord Spooky . . . . +5
...with Lord Spooky's signature . . . . +5
Escaping Spooky Manor through the Front Door . . . +10
Riding home on your bike, safe and sound . . . . +5
Finishing without saving . . . . +5

ビョウトウZ

Z·WaRD

fter receiving a cryptic message
rom your troubled sister, you
ndertake a rescue mission to save
er from a hospital of horrors.

SURVIVAL HO
EXPERIENCED
MATURE (16+)
CONTENT RATED BY M TRB

Z-WARD MAP

MENU

Z-WARD

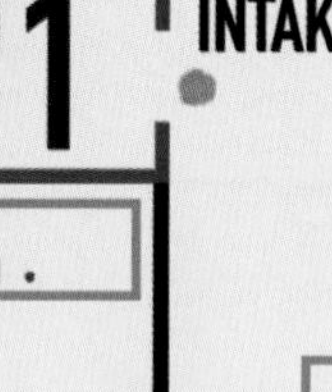

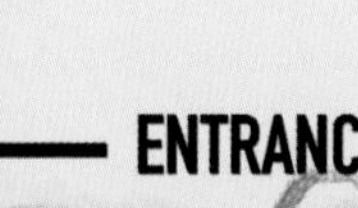

be careful!!

2
GROUP THERAPY
SLEEPING QUARTERS
1
INTAKE
ADMIN OFFICE
ENTRANCE
B
BASEMENT
STEAM TUNNELS
BOILER ROOM

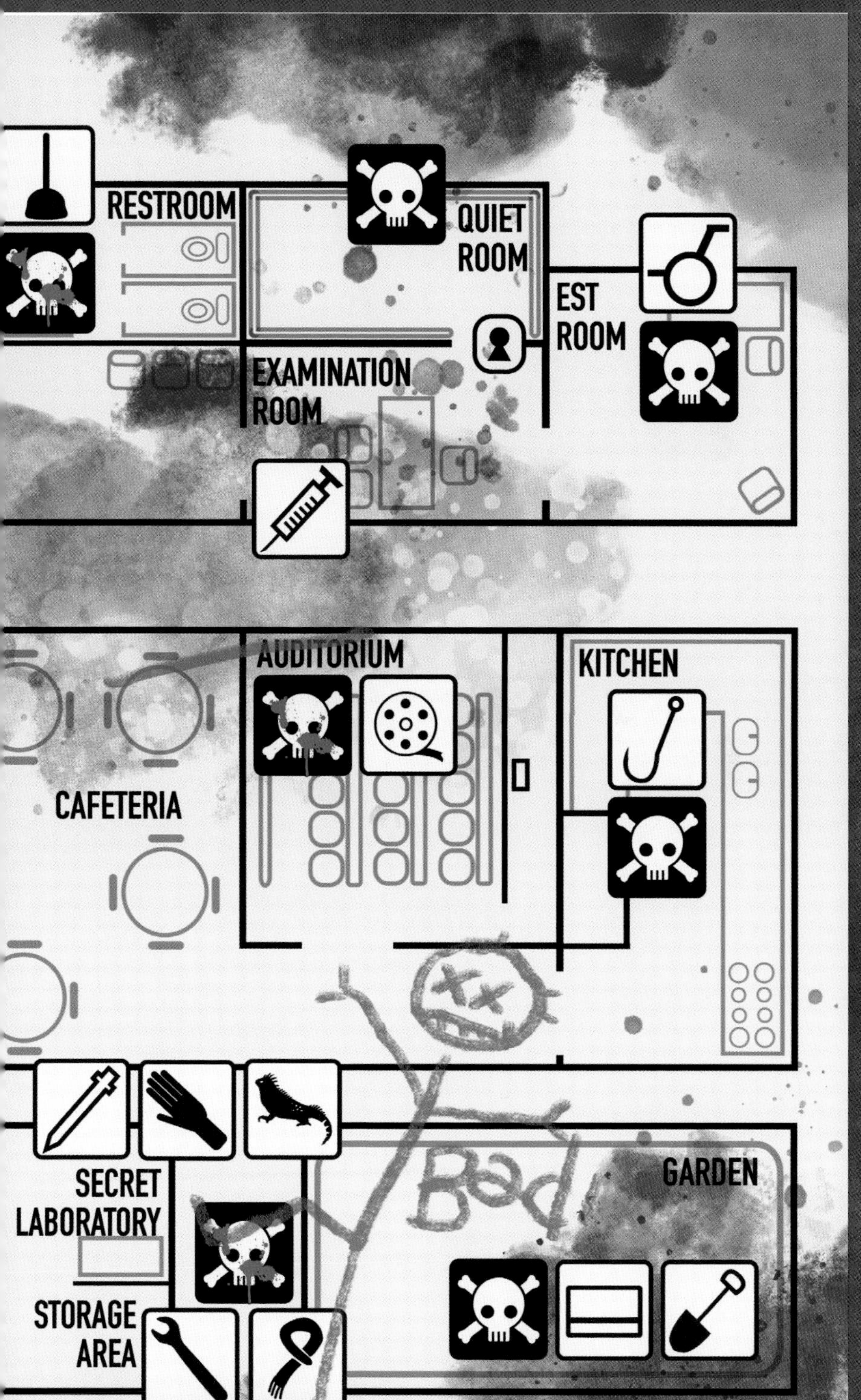
RESTROOM
QUIET
ROOM
EST
ROOM
EXAMINATION
ROOM
AUDITORIUM
KITCHEN
CAFETERIA
Bad
GARDEN
SECRET
LABORATORY
STORAGE
AREA

MENU

BACKSTORY

> FOR THE PARSER ONLY!

> Zombies overrun the hospital, and they hunger for flesh!

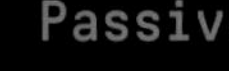

Rooms containing zombies are marked with skull symbols.

Passive zombies are represented by white skulls.

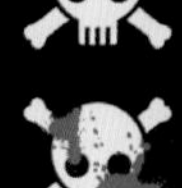

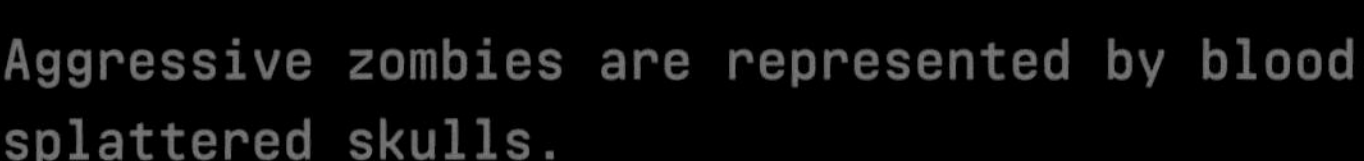

Aggressive zombies are represented by blood-splattered skulls.

> There are two kinds of zombies:

> Passive zombies are distracted or hindered. They will attack or pursue only if the player gets too close or provokes them.

> Aggressive zombies will attack and bite the player after *one* command is given. If the player leaves the room, they will pursue.

> Every zombie may be killed by the player with a single attack, save for the group of zombies in the auditorium. This large group cannot be killed, only pacified.

Rooms containing items are marked with appropriate item symbols.

ADVANCED RULES

> The Basement

> Want to give your players an even greater challenge? Add the Basement level for more zombies and more puzzles. Look for the Advanced Rules in the description of the Elevator (page 248).

HOSPITAL ENTRANCE

You're outside the hospital where your sister was admitted nine weeks ago. You may enter to the north. The hospital grounds continue east. You're holding a note.

EXAMINE NOTE: You read the poorly spelled email you received this morning from your sister:

"halp zomby apokalips xoxo frances"

Below that are your handwritten directions to this hospital.

HOSPITAL ENTRANCE exits are:

> NORTH page 247 HOSPITAL INTAKE
> EAST page 246 GARDENS

GARDENS

MENU

You are in the gardens. Someone's been digging graves. There is a shovel here. A man staggers nearby.

EXAMINE MAN: He is dressed in a white coat with a keycard clipped to the pocket. There is a ragged tear in his throat; blood is everywhere.

TALK TO MAN: The only person who should be talking to this man is a priest.

EXAMINE KEYCARD: The name on the keycard reads "Dr. Brent Honeycutt." There's a magnetic strip on the back.

> If the player entered the hospital before coming here, the man will have turned into a zombie.

EXAMINE MAN: You see a zombie fumbling with a keycard clipped to its bloody lab coat.

EXAMINE SHOVEL: It's a shovel, a staple of any good horror-themed scenario.

HIT ZOMBIE/MAN WITH SHOVEL: Bashing the poor man's head in breaks the handle of the shovel. The broken shovel and the man fall to the ground.

> Once the player deals with Dr. Honeycutt, they can GET KEYCARD.

GARDENS exits are:
> WEST page 245 HOSPITAL ENTRANCE

HOSPITAL INTAKE

You are in the hospital intake, where patients are admitted. A small fire extinguisher hangs on the blood-spattered wall. There is an elevator here. Stairs lead up. Doors lead south, west and east.

GO WEST: The office door is locked. You need a keycard to enter.

USE KEYCARD: The message "Authorized" is displayed on the reader, and you hear the door unlock.

EXAMINE FIRE EXTINGUISHER: This extinguisher contains carbon dioxide, a nonflammable gas. There's a warning on the label not to spray people with it.

USE FIRE EXTINGUISHER: The nozzle emits a blast of super cold CO_2.

> It will freeze any zombie in its path. It may be used only once.

ENTER ELEVATOR: A zombie claws at you from inside the elevator!

> The player has time to escape, but the zombie must be neutralized before the Elevator may be used.

HOSPITAL INTAKE exits are:

> SOUTH page 245 HOSPITAL ENTRANCE

> EAST page 250 CAFETERIA

⊡ WEST page 249 ADMINISTRATOR'S OFFICE

> UP page 254 GROUP THERAPY ROOM

⊡ ELEVATOR page 248 ELEVATOR

ELEVATOR

MENU

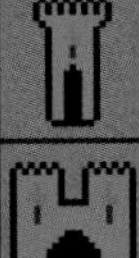

You are in the elevator. There is a control panel here.

EXAMINE PANEL: You see buttons for floors (1) and (2).

> PRESS 1 or PRESS 2 causes the doors to close, the Elevator to travel to that floor, then the doors to open. On the second floor, the Elevator opens to the Group Therapy Room (page 254). On the first floor, the Elevator opens to the Hospital Intake (page 247).

ADVANCED RULES

EXAMINE PANEL: You see buttons for floors (1) and (2), as well as a button marked (B) next to a keycard reader.

USE KEYCARD: The message "Unauthorized" is displayed on the reader.

> If the player has rescued Frances and tries to PRESS 1:

The doors open to reveal a horde of zombies blocking all the exits. Their hands reach for you, but the doors close just in time.

> If the player has rescued Frances and tries to PRESS B:

Frances reaches into her pocket and quietly hands you a blank keycard. She says, "You need this. I stole this from that mean man when he locked me up."

EXAMINE BLANK KEYCARD: The keycard has a magnetic strip on the back but no name.

USE BLANK KEYCARD: The message "Authorized" is displayed on the reader and the (B) button lights up.

PRESS B: You descend to the basement.

> The player goes to the Basement (page 261).

ELEVATOR exits are:

⊠ PRESS 1: page 247 HOSPITAL INTAKE
> PRESS 2: page 254 GROUP THERAPY ROOM
⊠ PRESS B: page 261 BASEMENT

ADMINISTRATOR'S OFFICE

You are in the administrator's office. There is a personal computer here. You recognize the chief of staff cowering in the corner behind a filing cabinet.

> The player can enter this room using Dr. Honeycutt's keycard.

EXAMINE CHIEF OF STAFF: The hysterical chief of staff yells, "Stay back! I'm warning you!" He holds a small revolver.

USE SYRINGE ON CHIEF OF STAFF: You rush the doctor and inject him with the syringe before he can react. He murmurs something unintelligible, then slumps to the floor.

> Although he's not a zombie, he will open fire unless he's sedated:

He panics and fires, hitting you in the chest. THE END.

SEARCH CHIEF OF STAFF: He is carrying a key and a revolver.

EXAMINE KEY: It's a simple padlock key.

EXAMINE REVOLVER: There's one bullet left.

EXAMINE COMPUTER: You read a memo about a drug designed to treat antisocial behavior. The hospital was selected to host the first trials of the drug.

EXAMINE FILING CABINET: You find your sister's file.

EXAMINE FILE: The file is stamped "Test Subject Z." It seems Frances "had trouble adjusting" and was sent to the quiet room.

ADMINISTRATOR'S OFFICE exits are:

> OUT page 247 HOSPITAL INTAKE

CAFETERIA

You are standing in a large cafeteria. Flies buzz around half-eaten trays of food. Several corpses litter the floor. The kitchen is to the east. Lights flicker within a dark room to the north.

> If the power is out, the player hears flies buzzing around and smells spoiled food.

EXAMINE TRAYS: Looks like it was meatloaf day.

EXAMINE CORPSES: They're dead. They're all messed up.

CAFETERIA exits are:

> NORTH page 252 AUDITORIUM

> EAST page 251 KITCHEN

> WEST page 247 HOSPITAL INTAKE

KITCHEN

You are in the hospital's kitchen. There's a meat hook next to a meat grinder.

A zombie claws at the door of a walk-in refrigerator.

EXAMINE MEAT HOOK: A hook used to grab sides of meat.

EXAMINE WALK-IN: A zombie is trying to get inside.

> Once the player deals with the zombie, they can open the refrigerator.

USE MEAT HOOK ON ZOMBIE: You pierce its brain and it falls down. The hook is now stuck.

OPEN WALK-IN: You open the heavy door and find a chef shivering inside.

EXAMINE CHEF: She's wearing a white apron and a nametag that reads "Chef Peggy."

TALK TO CHEF: She asks, "You didn't eat anything, did you?"

ASK CHEF ABOUT MEATLOAF/VITAMIN Z: "The chief of staff told me to add Vitamin Z to the meatloaf. He said it would help calm down the more difficult patients. After that, everything just went to hell."

> After being rescued, she'll follow the player out to the Cafeteria and then flee the hospital.

KITCHEN exits are:
> WEST page 250 CAFETERIA

AUDITORIUM

MENU

The theater is filled with the shuffling bodies of zombified patients and staff members! The light from a film projector illuminates a large screen. A short set of stairs leads up to the projector room.

There are too many zombies to fight. Upon seeing you, they become agitated and start to close in...

EXAMINE SCREEN: The screen is blank, illuminated by the bright light of an empty film projector.

> If the power is out, the player can sneak past the shuffling zombies to the Projector Room (page 253).

AUDITORIUM exits are:

> SOUTH page 250 CAFETERIA
> UP page 253 PROJECTOR ROOM

PROJECTOR ROOM

You're standing by an electrical panel on the wall next to a film projector. Pete, the orderly, is here. There are two film reels here.

> If the power is out, emergency lighting allows the player to see.

EXAMINE PETE: Pete wears the white uniform of a hospital orderly. "I've been hiding in here for days!"

> If the power goes out while Pete is still in this room, he'll reset the circuit breakers.

EXAMINE PROJECTOR: It's an old-fashioned movie projector.

EXAMINE FILM REELS: You note two classic movies: *Bambi* and *Night of the Living Dead.*

> The film reels may be spooled onto the projector; they're too cumbersome to carry.

PLAY BAMBI: The zombies become enraged when Bambi's mother dies and they break down the door, killing everyone inside. THE END.

PLAY NIGHT OF THE LIVING DEAD: The zombies return to their seats to watch the movie.

> It's now safe to leave the Projector Room.

EXAMINE ELECTRICAL PANEL: You see a master reset switch for the circuit breakers.

RESET CIRCUIT BREAKERS: The lights flicker back on as power is restored.

PROJECTOR ROOM exits are:
⊠ OUT page 252 AUDITORIUM

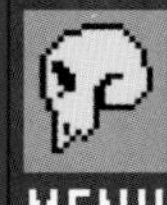
MENU

GROUP THERAPY ROOM

You are in the group therapy room. Stairs lead down. There's an elevator here. You see a bathroom to the north and exits to the east and west.

There is a zombie here, watching television with its mouth wide open.

> If the TV is turned off, the zombie gets up and attacks the player!

WATCH TELEVISION: A blonde woman on screen is reporting from outside a wrought-iron gate. In the distance is a large manor. "Authorities investigate report of missing courier..."

> The player cannot go down the stairs while pushing Frances in the wheelchair. The player and Frances must take the Elevator instead.

GROUP THERAPY ROOM exits are:
> NORTH page 256 RESTROOM
> EAST page 257 EXAMINATION ROOM
> WEST page 255 SLEEPING QUARTERS
> DOWN page 247 HOSPITAL INTAKE
> ELEVATOR page 248 ELEVATOR

SLEEPING QUARTERS

This dimly lit room is filled with small cots.

EXAMINE COTS: Beneath a cot is a stuffed bunny and a chalk drawing on the tiled floor.

EXAMINE BUNNY: You gave this to your sister before she went away.

EXAMINE DRAWING: It's a child's drawing of an iguana. The name "Lulu" is written next to it.

SLEEPING QUARTERS exits are:
> OUT page 254 GROUP THERAPY ROOM

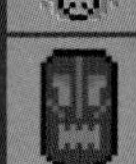

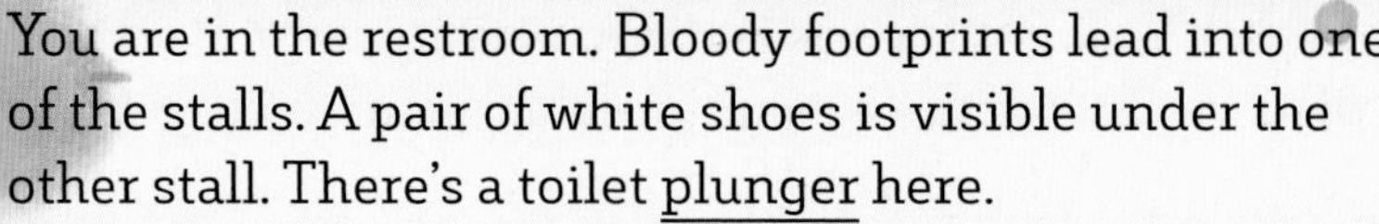

RESTROOM

You are in the restroom. Bloody footprints lead into one of the stalls. A pair of white shoes is visible under the other stall. There's a toilet plunger here.

GET PLUNGER: As you grab the plunger, a zombie bursts out of a stall with its pants around its ankles.

The pants-less zombie lunges for your throat!

USE PLUNGER ON ZOMBIE: The plunger sticks to the zombie's face, rendering it harmless.

EXAMINE STALL: You see a pair of feet in nurse's shoes. A voice asks, "Is it safe to come out?"

ASK NURSE ABOUT MEATLOAF/VITAMIN Z: "I'm vegan. I don't eat meatloaf."

ASK NURSE ABOUT QUIET ROOM: "It's just down the hall. You'll need a key to get in."

> Once rescued, the nurse follows the player out of the Restroom and makes her escape to the Hospital Entrance.

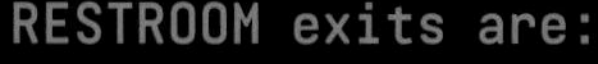

RESTROOM exits are:

> OUT page 254 GROUP THERAPY ROOM

EXAMINATION ROOM

You are in one of the hospital's examination rooms. At the north side of the room is a padlocked door with a sign on it. There is a syringe here. Exits are to the east and west.

EXAMINE SIGN: It reads "Quiet Room."

ENTER QUIET ROOM: It's locked.

> The padlock can be unlocked with the chief of staff's key. The player can also use the fire extinguisher on the lock to freeze and break the padlock, assuming there's any CO_2 left.

EXAMINE SYRINGE: The syringe contains a powerful sedative.

> The syringe can be used once; it doesn't affect zombies.

EXAMINATION ROOM exits are:

⊠ NORTH page 258 QUIET ROOM
> EAST page 259 ELECTROSHOCK THERAPY (EST) ROOM
> WEST page 254 GROUP THERAPY ROOM

QUIET ROOM

MENU

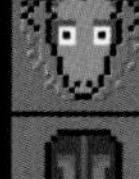
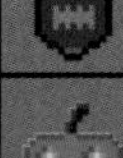

You stand in a padded cell where the more difficult patients are kept. One of the wall panels has a deep rip in the padding.

A straitjacketed zombie is here, staring off into space.

EXAMINE WALL: Someone or something tore out the panel and clumsily replaced it.

REMOVE PANEL: You pull the panel out of the wall, revealing a secret compartment. Your sister, Frances, is hiding inside!

EXAMINE FRANCES: Frances is weak, dehydrated and terrified.

> She will not leave her hiding space unless the player GIVES BUNNY TO FRANCES. Once Frances emerges from the secret compartment, she collapses into the player's arms. She must be placed in the wheelchair and wheeled to the Hospital Entrance via the Elevator.

> If the player leaves Frances in this room without securing her back in her hiding place and replacing the wall panel:

After you leave, the straitjacketed zombie attacks Frances! You manage to escape Z-Ward with your life but you'll never forgive yourself for the loss of your sister. THE END.

QUIET ROOM exits are:

> OUT page 257 EXAMINATION ROOM

EST ROOM

You're in the electroshock therapy room. A zombie is strapped into a wheelchair. Electrodes run from its skull to a nearby machine.

> The zombie is strapped in and cannot attack… for now.

EXAMINE WHEELCHAIR: The wheelchair is old but in good condition.

> The wheelchair cannot be used with the zombie strapped into it.

EXAMINE ZOMBIE: The zombie is strapped into the wheelchair. Electrodes from the EST machine are attached to its skull.

EXAMINE EST MACHINE: It's used to administer electrical currents to the patient's brain. You see a dial with four settings: Off, Low, Medium and High. It's currently set to Off.

SET DIAL TO LOW: The machine hums, but the zombie seems unaffected.

SET DIAL TO MEDIUM: The machine hums, the lights flicker and the zombie jerks around. It looks dazed, unaware of its surroundings.

> The stunned zombie may be removed from the chair, but it will recover quickly.

ELECTROSHOCK THERAPY (EST) ROOM exits are:

> OUT page 257 EXAMINATION ROOM

EST ROOM (CONTINUED)

SET DIAL TO HIGH: The machine hums, and the zombie thrashes around. Something goes wrong: the machine starts to smoke and the electrodes catch fire! The zombie's eyes burst from their sockets and the power goes out!

> While the power is out, the player cannot see—but neither can the zombies. Exits and objects may still be used.

> If Pete, the orderly, hasn't been rescued, Pete resets the circuit breaker from the projection booth:

After a few seconds of darkness, the lights flicker back on.

> If Pete was rescued, nobody's there to reset the circuit breaker. The player must navigate the Hospital in total darkness, get to the Projector Room and restore power.

BASEMENT

You're in the basement. You see the entrance to the steam tunnels. A mop and bucket are by the elevator.

EXAMINE BUCKET: The bucket is filled with relatively clean water. It's on wheels and can be pushed around.

TAKE BUCKET: It's quite heavy; it will spill if you carry it around.

> The mop does no damage but can be used to push a zombie out of the way, allowing the player to take any exit from a room. The zombie will follow the player and attack if given the opportunity.

BASEMENT exits are:

> EAST page 262 STEAM TUNNELS
> ELEVATOR page 248 ELEVATOR

STEAM TUNNELS

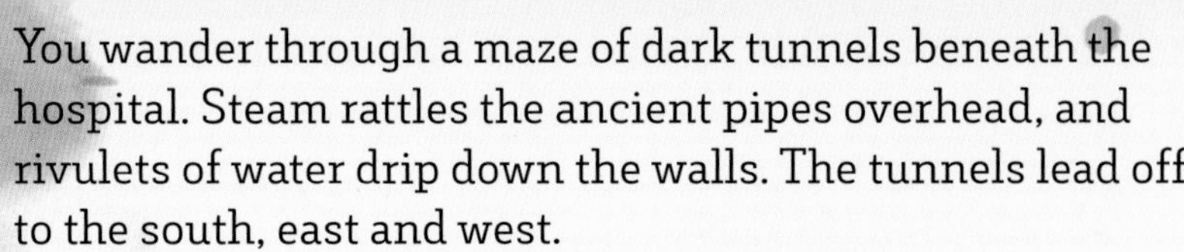

You wander through a maze of dark tunnels beneath the hospital. Steam rattles the ancient pipes overhead, and rivulets of water drip down the walls. The tunnels lead off to the south, east and west.

> A zombie will wander into the tunnels after the player enters the Secret Lab. When they return to the steam tunnels:

You see a zombie. It staggers toward you, holding the bloody stump where its hand once was.

> The zombie blocks the tunnel leading to the Boiler Room. The player can KILL ZOMBIE WITH WRENCH, KILL ZOMBIE WITH TROCAR or PUSH ZOMBIE WITH MOP.

GIVE HAND TO ZOMBIE: Confused, the zombie stares at the hand. It looks stumped.

> The zombie will be distracted long enough for the player to escape the Steam Tunnels.

STEAM TUNNELS exits are:

⊠ SOUTH page 265 BOILER ROOM

> EAST page 263 SECRET LAB

> WEST page 261 BASEMENT

SECRET LAB

You are in a makeshift laboratory. There's a hospital gurney against one wall and a large freezer standing against the other. The steam tunnels are to the west. A storage area is to the south.

EXAMINE GURNEY: You see a severed hand hanging from the gurney by a pair of handcuffs. A medical instrument rests on the gurney.

EXAMINE INSTRUMENT: The word of the day is "trocar": a hollow steel implement with a sharp end, used to drain bodily fluids during surgery or embalming.

MOVE GURNEY: One of the wheels pops off and rolls along the ground. This thing is falling apart and won't be of much use to you.

EXAMINE FREEZER: It's big enough to hold a couple of people... or parts of a couple of people. The freezer contains a plastic bag.

EXAMINE BAG: The plastic bag is labeled "Lulu," and it contains a frozen iguana.

EXAMINE IGUANA: She's dead, wrapped in plastic.

> Lulu the Iguana is worth bonus points if given to Frances.

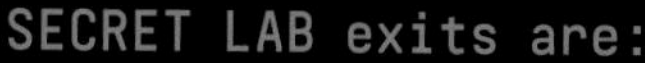

SECRET LAB exits are:

> SOUTH page 264 STORAGE AREA
> WEST page 262 STEAM TUNNELS

STORAGE AREA

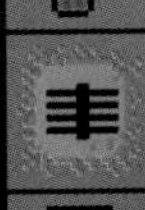

This room is piled high with old suitcases and boxes of medical records. A zombie clad in work coveralls turns to look at you with dead eyes. It holds a monkey wrench.

> The zombie swings the wrench wildly and will then try to bite the player.

KILL ZOMBIE WITH TROCAR: You stab the zombie in the brain with the trocar. It spurts blood and brain fluid. The zombie drops the monkey wrench and keels over.

EXAMINE MONKEY WRENCH: A large metal wrench used to adjust pipe fittings.

EXAMINE MEDICAL RECORDS: You don't have time to go through 40 years of paperwork.

EXAMINE SUITCASES: There are a few dozen suitcases stacked to the ceiling. Rummaging through them reveals some old clothing.

EXAMINE CLOTHING: The clothes are very old, possibly belonging to former patients. You find a pair of cool vintage scarves.

EXAMINE SCARVES: Perfect! One for you, one for Frances.

STORAGE AREA exits are:

> OUT page 263 SECRET LAB

BOILER ROOM

The hospital's antique boiler sits directly below the hospital entrance. A few steel drums stand in the corner. The room reeks of chemicals. The steam tunnels are north of here.

> If the player isn't wearing a soaked scarf:

The fumes make you feel light-headed...

> If the player is wearing a soaked scarf:

Your scarf filters out the fumes and you can breathe easier.

EXAMINE DRUMS: A warning reads: "Extremely flammable. Do not use without adequate ventilation." One of the drums is leaking volatile chemicals onto the floor.

Frances coughs and presses her face into her bunny's fur.

TAKE DRUMS: They're too heavy to move.

EXAMINE BOILER: This boiler heats the entire hospital. It's old and in need of repair. You see some pressure gauges and a safety valve.

EXAMINE GAUGES: The boiler's pressure seems to be at a safe level.

EXAMINE SAFETY VALVE: It's old and rusty.

TURN SAFETY VALVE: It's stuck in the "on" position.

BOILER ROOM exits are:

> OUT page 262 STEAM TUNNELS

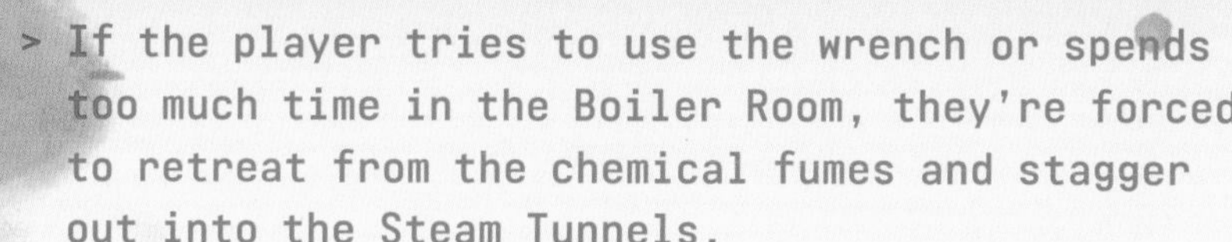

BOILER ROOM (CONTINUED)

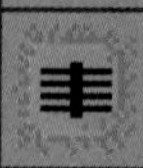

> If the player tries to use the wrench or spends too much time in the Boiler Room, they're forced to retreat from the chemical fumes and stagger out into the Steam Tunnels.

> The player must WET SCARF in water from the Restroom or the mop bucket, then WEAR SCARF to filter out the fumes.

> The player can escape by blowing up the Boiler Room, killing the zombies directly above it. Once the valve is turned off, the player and Frances must get out as soon as possible.

USE WRENCH ON SAFETY VALVE: With great effort, you manage to shut off the safety valve.

The boiler begins to rattle and hiss as the pressure rises.

> The danger increases with each turn spent in the Basement level:

Steam begins to build up in the boiler.

> The player and Frances should be in the lab or Basement by now.

The gauges climb into the red zone. Boiling steam hisses from the pipes.

> This is the last chance to get to the safety of the Elevator or the freezer.

The boiler explodes, igniting the chemical drums, and sends a fireball shooting up from beneath the hospital!

> If the player and Frances hide in the lab's freezer or in the Elevator, they're safe. If not:

You and your sister perish in the fiery explosion. THE END.

ESCAPING FROM THE HOSPITAL

> As the player and Frances retrace their steps to the Hospital Entrance, describe each room as filled with burning, smoking debris and other wreckage from the blast. Upon leaving the Elevator on the first floor:

You emerge from the elevator into a scene of utter chaos and carnage. Pieces of charred, smoking zombies litter the ground. Frances shakily stands up from the wheelchair and hugs you tight. Finally free from this nightmare, the two of you step out into the bright sunlight and leave Z-Ward behind... forever. THE END.

INVENTORY CHECKLIST

These items may be carried by the player:

- [x] Note
- [ ] Shovel
- [ ] Dr. Honeycutt's keycard
- [ ] Fire extinguisher
- [ ] Key
- [ ] Revolver
- [ ] File
- [ ] Meat hook
- [ ] Stuffed bunny
- [ ] Plunger
- [ ] Syringe
- [ ] Wheelchair

These items may be acquired if you are using the Advanced Rules:

- [ ] Blank keycard
- [ ] Mop
- [ ] Severed hand
- [ ] Trocar
- [ ] Iguana
- [ ] Monkey wrench
- [ ] Scarves

SCORING

The player can earn a maximum of 100 points using the normal rules:

Reading the note..+5
Killing Dr. Honeycutt before he turns into a zombie .+5
Rescuing Pete from the Projector Room............+10
Rescuing Chef Peggy from the Kitchen ....+10
Rescuing the nurse from the Restroom ....+10
Sedating the chief of staff..............................+5
Retrieving your sister's file from the office ....+5
Not causing a power outage in the EST Room ....+5
Finding Frances inside the Quiet Room wall.......+10
Getting Frances to the Elevator.......................+5
Escaping from the hospital ....+25
Finishing without saving ....+5

BONUS POINTS

The player can earn +20 bonus points if using the Advanced Rules.

Descending to the Basement..........................+5
Giving the zombie back its severed hand............+5
Giving Frances Lulu the Iguana ....+5
Blowing up the boiler.....................................+5

ABOUT THE AUTHOR

Jared was introduced to text adventures by his sixth grade teacher, Mike Lipinski, who took his class on a field trip to Infocom (the publisher of *Zork*, *Planetfall* and many other text adventure games). In fact, Jared's first experience working in the game industry was as a beta tester for *Seastalker*, Infocom's underwater-themed "junior adventure game."

He published the first Parsely game, *Action Castle*, in 2009—about six years after creating it as an improvised game during a friend's game party. Jared's other game design credits include several tabletop roleplaying games (*InSpectres, Lacuna Part I, octaNe* and *FreeMarket*) and computer games (*Petz 3, Immortal Cities: Children of the Nile, Dungeons & Dragons Online: Stormreach* and *Lord of the Rings Online: Shadows of Angmar).*

MENU

INDEX

INDEX

INDEX

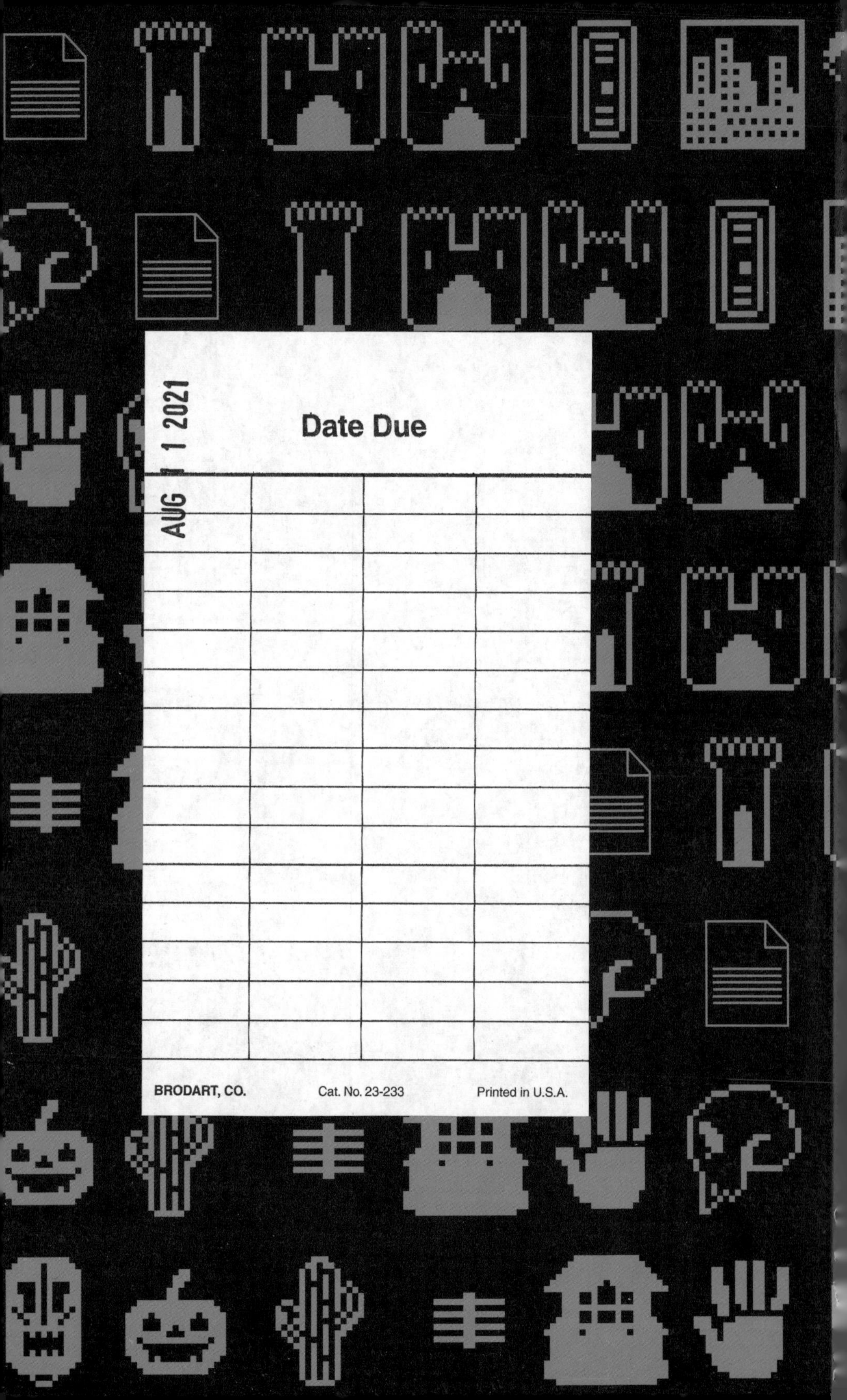
AUG 11 2021
Date Due
BRODART, CO.
Cat. No. 23-233
Printed in U.S.A.